J. S. BACH'S
CHROMATIC FANTASY
AND FUGUE

LONGMAN MUSIC SERIES

Series Editor: Gerald Warfield

J. S. BACH'S
CHROMATIC FANTASY
AND FUGUE

Critical Edition with Commentary

Heinrich Schenker

Translated and Edited by Hedi Siegel

Longman
New York & London

J. S. BACH'S CHROMATIC FANTASY AND FUGUE

Longman Inc., 1560 Broadway, New York, N.Y. 10036
Associated companies, branches, and representatives
throughout the world.

Revision © 1969 by Universal Edition A. G. Wien.

The English language edition has been authorized
by Universal Edition A. G.

Developmental Editor: Gordon T. R. Anderson
Editorial and Production Supervisor: Ferne Y. Kawahara

Composition: Graphicraft Typesetters

Library of Congress Cataloging in Publication Data
Schenker, Heinrich, 1868-1935.
  J. S. Bach, Chromatic fantasy and fugue.
  (Longman music series)
  "Works of Heinrich Schenker": p.
  1. Bach, Johann Sebastian, 1685-1750. Chromatische
Fantasie und Fuge. 2. Canons, fugues, etc. (Harpsi-
chord) I. Siegel, Hedi. II. Bach, Johann Sebastian,
1685-1750. Chromatische Fantasie und Fuge. 1984.
III. Title. IV. Title: Chromatic fantasy and fugue.
V. Series.
ML410.B13S343 1984   786.1'092'4   83-13638
ISBN 0-582-28330-2

Manufactured in the United States of America
Printing: 9 8 7 6 5 4 3 2 1   Year: 92 91 90 89 88 87 86 85 84

Contents

Note: Heinrich Schenker's edition of J.S. Bach's Chromatic Fantasy and Fugue is also provided in a separate score as a supplement to this volume.

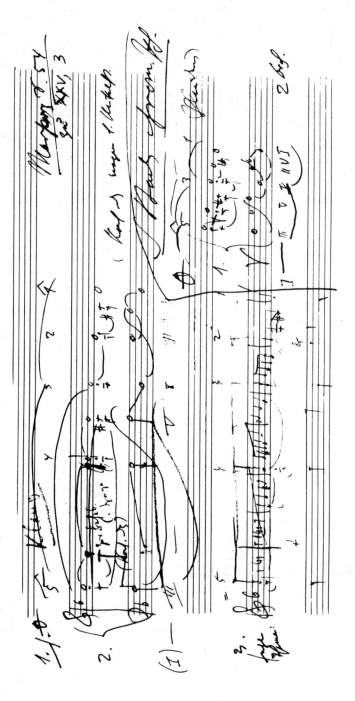

Plate I

Schenker's sketch of the opening of the Fugue, ca. 1928; see note 67 of the Commentary. (Reproduced by courtesy of the Oster Collection at the Music Division of the New York Public Library, Astor, Lenox, and Tilden Foundations.)

Translator's Foreword

Schenker's critical edition of Bach's Chromatic Fantasy and Fugue appeared at the end of the first decade of this century—a productive decade for Schenker. In 1906, he launched his major theoretical work, *Neue musikalische Theorien und Phantasien*, with the publication of *Harmonielehre*, the first book in the series. By 1910 the second book, *Kontrapunkt* (Part I), had already appeared. Among the editions and arrangements that Schenker issued in this period was his collection of C.P.E. Bach's keyboard works. Published in 1902, it was followed in 1904 by *Ein Beitrag zur Ornamentik* (revised in 1908), a work with close ties to the C.P.E. Bach edition.[1] At the end of the decade he probably began work on his unpublished study "Die Kunst des Vortrags."[2]

During these years, as throughout his life, he also remained an active practical musician and teacher, giving private lessons in piano and theory. By all accounts he was an extraordinary pedagogue,[3] and he certainly regarded the teaching of performing musicians as a central pursuit. Much of what he wrote grew out of ideas he wished to impart to performers—ideas that far exceeded the conventional methodology of practical and theoretical instruction. His critical editions with commentary (*Erläuterungen*)—of Bach's Chromatic Fantasy and Fugue and of the late piano sonatas of Beethoven—offer their readers the privilege of studying these works as if under Schenker's unique personal tutelage.

Schenker believed that every aspect of performance must grow out of an understanding of the true content of the music itself. The primary prerequisite for such an understanding was a score that remained faithful to the composer's intent. In the early part of this century, hardly any performing editions fulfilled this requirement, and few performers and teachers consulted the available scholarly editions. Schenker was surely not exaggerating when he wrote, in a letter to Ernst Rudorff dating from 1908: "I am the only teacher in Vienna who has his students use exclusively 'Urtext'

---

1. Bibliographic details for Schenker's publications are given in the Appendix: Works of Heinrich Schenker.

2. See note 111 of the Commentary.

3. Hans Wolf, a conductor who studied with Schenker, published some of his recollections and notes in "Schenkers Persönlichkeit im Unterricht," *Der Dreiklang*, Heft 7 (October, 1937), pp. 176-84.

and original editions, insofar as they are available."[4] Schenker must have felt that a presentation of the composer's original notation was particularly necessary in the case of the Chromatic Fantasy, for the widely used editions of this work were especially fanciful. Such editors as Ferruccio Busoni and Hans von Bülow did not hesitate to alter rhythms, add notes and dynamic markings, and insert their own copious instructions to the performer. Schenker devotes a considerable portion of his commentary to a refutation of these capricious editorial alterations; his justification of the original reading often provides valuable insight into the musical meaning of the passage in question. Since the autograph was no longer extant, he based his edition on that of the Bach-Gesellschaft. In explaining his choice between variant readings, Schenker likewise provides musical insight, for his arguments go beyond philological comparison.

Besides commenting on the interpretations found in various editions, Schenker offers his thoughts on a wide range of subjects, all suggested by the inner content of the composition. Even his views on the practical aspects of performing technique[5]—such as fingering and touch—grow out of a study of the music itself, for it was his belief that technique was meaningless if applied mechanically. In an important section on dynamics, one of the special sections in the commentary, he puts forward an idea that was to be taken up again a few years later in his monograph on the Ninth Symphony: that the dynamic interpretation of a composition is predetermined by its musical content.

Schenker's writings of the first decade of the century represent an early stage in his development; thus his commentary by no means constitutes a complete analysis of either the Fantasy or the Fugue.[6] Often his analytic insights point to later writings. His discussion of the improvisatory aspect of the Fantasy demonstrates his intimate familiarity with C.P.E. Bach's writings and is directly linked to his later essay, "Die Kunst der Improvisation" (*Das Meisterwerk in der Musik, Jahrbuch* I, 1925). His description of the Fugue's structure, however valuable, cannot be considered a true analysis of a fugue; such was to come later in "Das Organische der Fuge," published in the second *Jahrbuch* of *Das Meisterwerk in der Musik* (1926). His harmonic readings of several passages reflect the early stage of his thought as delineated in *Harmonielehre*. And the *Urlinie* concept is only hinted at—in his discussions of the recitative section of the Fantasy and the opening of the Fugue, for example.

Schenker returned to the Chromatic Fantasy and Fugue in his later writings. *Der freie Satz* contains a graph and some discussion of the opening bars of the Fugue.[7] This late graph is the product of Schenker's continuing reflection on the work.

---

4. The letter is transcribed by Oswald Jonas in "Ein textkritisches Problem der Ballade op. 38 von Frédéric Chopin," *Acta Musicologica*, vol. 35 (1963), pp. 156–57; see note 6 of the Introduction.

5. Schenker's remarks presuppose performance of the work on the modern piano; he makes no reference to earlier keyboard instruments.

6. Schenker's critics often fail to take this into account; see especially Ludwig Czaczkes, *Bachs Chromatische Fantasie und Fuge* (Vienna: Österreichischer Bundesverlag für Unterricht, Wissenschaft und Kunst, 1971).

7. See note 67 of the Commentary.

Several sketches pertaining to the Fantasy and the Fugue are preserved in the Oster Collection, now housed in the Music Division of the New York Public Library, Special Collections. One of these sketches, which appears to be a direct antecedent of the published graph of the Fugue's opening, is reproduced in facsimile in plate I (facing the start of this Foreword). I have included material from a few of the other sketches in the notes to the commentary.

Also preserved in the Oster Collection is Schenker's personal copy of his critical edition of the Chromatic Fantasy and Fugue in its published form—Ernst Oster's catalogue (typewritten in German) lists it as "Schenkers Handexemplar." Both the score and the commentary contain annotations in Schenker's hand; these are especially plentiful in the score and include detailed markings pertaining to both performance and analysis (often inseparable): dynamic signs, rubato arrows, slurs, phrase marks, additional or alternate fingerings, lines connecting lengthened stems, figured-bass numbers, Roman numerals, and letter names of notes to indicate bass progressions (frequently corresponding to the analytic remarks included in the printed commentary). In one instance Schenker marked an obvious omission; this has been corrected in the present print of the score.[8] There is no indication of how soon after publication these annotations were entered, but some, which contain revisions of the harmonic schemes presented in the commentary, show a somewhat later stage of Schenker's harmonic thinking than that found in *Harmonielehre*. Though not intended for publication, some of these sketches are of great interest; transcriptions have been included in the notes to the commentary where it seemed appropriate. The notes also contain references to the other types of annotations, but I have not attempted to give a comprehensive presentation of Schenker's markings. A considerable number were obviously jotted down as personal reminders; written in very faint pencil and in abbreviated form, they are often very difficult to decipher.

Completed in 1909, Schenker's edition of the Chromatic Fantasy and Fugue appeared in print in 1910, published by Universal Edition in Vienna. In 1969 it was reissued in a revised edition by Oswald Jonas as part of Universal Edition's Wiener Urtext Ausgabe series. Jonas left Schenker's score and commentary intact (correcting a few misprints) and added five footnotes that refer the reader to a new page of annotations. (The original and revised editions bear the same plate number: U.E. 2540.) In this translation, two of Jonas's footnote references have been moved to locations in the text that seemed more appropriate. Schenker's own annotations, originally parenthetical references within the text, appear as notes, with amplified bibliographic information. The reference numbers of Schenker's and Jonas's notes are marked with an asterisk to differentiate them from my own annotations. These new annotations, as well as my additions to Schenker's and Jonas's notes, are set off by square brackets: [ ]. Translations appearing within the notes are mine unless otherwise indicated. The examples in Schenker's commentary have been numbered for ease of reference. In general, the few misprints that appeared within the examples and in the text of the commentary have been corrected without comment.

My annotations could not have been completed without the help of John Rothgeb, by whose courtesy I obtained the information relevant to this translation held by the Oster Collection (access is restricted as of this writing). I am further indebted to him

---

8. See note 62 of the Commentary.

for his careful check of the entire translation and his inspired solutions to countless problems. I owe special thanks to Carl Schachter for the encouragement, guidance, and invaluable advice he gave me while the translation was in progress and after he read the completed manuscript. I am also especially grateful to Larry Laskowski and Channan Willner, who gave the manuscript their close attention and made many important suggestions.

Hedi Siegel
New York, 1984

Preface

The sources on which this edition is based are described in the Introduction.

A brief word on the dynamic markings:

All of the *crescendo* and *diminuendo* signs (———— and ————►) are mine. In the first part of the work—in the Fantasy—some of the dynamic indications are Bach's original markings while others (those in parentheses) have been added by me.* In the second part—in the Fugue—all of the dynamic indications are mine.

Heinrich Schenker
Vienna, September 1909

[*By "Bach's original markings" Schenker meant those given in the Bach-Gesellschaft edition. Schenker did add some of his own dynamic signs to the Fantasy, but the parentheses he intended for them never appeared in print (see notes 1 and 2 of the Introduction). At the end of his commentary, he discussed his addition of dynamic markings and addressed the subject of dynamics in general.]

CHROMATIC FANTASY
AND FUGUE*

J.S. BACH

*The variant reading of the Fantasy has an entirely different beginning.

[**N.B. Throughout this score, bar numbers appear at the *end* of the numbered measures.]

1

[**See note 62 of the Commentary.]

FUGA.

9

*possibly:

CHROMATIC FANTASY
Variant*

[*See the Commentary (the discussion of bar 3 of the Fantasy) and note 12.]

Introduction

The chief source for the present edition is the edition issued by the Bach-Gesellschaft.[1] Since the autograph is no longer extant,[2] this printed source has no greater authority than a copyist's manuscript; therefore it had to be given the most careful critical scrutiny. In the interest of textual accuracy, I felt it my duty to consult the more important current editions as well.[3]

My edition departs from that of the Bach-Gesellschaft at several points. For example, a different reading may be found in the Fantasy, bar 50, and in the Fugue, bar 85 (right- and left-hand parts).

Furthermore, this edition offers what I believe to be the definitive reading at many of those points where the editors of the Bach-Gesellschaft failed to decide between two alternative versions. Bars 5 and 25 of the Fantasy may serve as two examples.

If my criticism of the other editions in the main seems disparaging, the detailed explanation provided in my commentary (*Erläuterungen*) will serve to refute any charge that my veneration of Bach is mere blind worship.

One may surely assume that even the most renowned editors, such men as Bülow and Reinecke, must have had an initial awareness of the gulf that separates them from Bach; their ardent admiration of this master must have led them to cast aside any envy or argument and readily acknowledge the superiority of his artistic instinct. What could therefore have induced them, when called upon to edit a work by J. S. Bach, suddenly to forget their humility, negate their trust in Bach's superior artistry, and allow themselves to make so many offensive emendations—more often than not in those very passages where Bach's genius is most evident?

Since it is inconceivable that they were motivated by *mala fides* or petty vanity, only one conclusion is possible (indeed, what else could one think?): in spite of their respect for Bach, they nevertheless regarded their own versions as artistically superior to the composer's original settings.

Viewed in this context, my commentary aims to reveal the true compositional basis of the original setting. May it also demonstrate that such inner understanding became inaccessible to editors the moment they began to tamper with the original. Yet I cherish the hope that my explanation of musical techniques is no mere lifeless philological criticism; indeed, I am quite certain that I have done the reader and performer a practical service whose value should not be underestimated, since only this kind of detailed study enables one to perform or understand a work in its true meaning!

And perhaps those who show some interest in these matters would benefit even further if they were finally to fathom the immense gulf that separates a genius such as Bach from other musicians, no matter how famous (e.g., Bülow or Reinecke). If they would only realize that, compared to Bach's, the musical instincts of such men (amply demonstrated by the examples of their editorial work given in my commentary) are no different from the ordinary and common instincts of so-called "musical" people. When this kind of musician uses the modest dimensions of his own instincts as a yardstick for the immeasurable instincts of a master, he immediately reveals either his own severe ignorance or his unforgivable arrogance!

Both those who create and those who re-create would be well served by an essay (which perhaps would merit a separate monograph) showing that composers, be they J. S. Bach or C.P.E. Bach, Beethoven or Chopin, are always right—in all that they wrote and in the way they wrote it!—that they are impervious to the challenges of Bülow, Klindworth, Riemann, Scholz, etc., who think they know better and attempt to correct them. A higher musical level would be attained if musicians could finally confront the original text—if they could at least see for themselves and gain new acquaintance of those priceless details of content and notation which, because of ignorance, have been extirpated by so many editors. This would allow for the possibility that many musicians, either by instinct or by chance, might evaluate those details more correctly than the editors themselves—and surely the first prerequisite for such an evaluation is access to the original. Who has the right—who could dare—to misrepresent the original text? To draw a parallel with the other arts: would a bold falsification of a text by Goethe or a painting by Rembrandt remain unchallenged? In the domain of poetry, there is a strict concern for the preservation of the poet's language, at any cost, regardless of such hazards as the momentary political or ethical implications of the written word. In the domain of music such hazards are excluded; yet it is in this very domain that the requisite fidelity to the original is so strangely absent, the proper concern for truth so lacking. Editors profess that they know better than composers and readily substitute their own ideas! These editors lack the faintest inkling of the obvious notion that they would do much better to edit their own works, or those of second- and third-rate composers, instead of the compositions of those very masters who—as one can imagine—need editing least of all! As a result, when faced with these many editions, it is hard to decide whether one should express horror at the editors' ignorance or deplore their stupidity!

Those who do not search for reasons—who suffer from the age-old affliction of so-called "musical" people, which leads them always to assume, when in doubt, that the error lies with Bach or Beethoven rather than with a famous conductor or pedagogue they call a "genius"—should be guided by the thoughts of such masters as Mendelssohn or Brahms on this subject.

In a letter to Moscheles (dated March 7, 1845), Mendelssohn writes:

> On less important points I am ready to give way; as, for instance, in reference to the accidentals—although there, too, I prefer the old method, on account of the long bars. But I cannot possibly introduce my marks of expression into a score of Handel's, nor my tempi, nor anything else, unless it is to be made perfectly clear what is mine and what Handel's; and as he has put his pianos and fortes and his figured basses where he thought them necessary, I must either omit

them or leave the public in doubt as to which is his marking and which mine. It would be no great trouble *to any one who agrees with my marking*, to have it copied from the pianoforte arrangement into the score. On the other hand, it would be no slight evil if the edition did not clearly distinguish between Handel's and the editor's views. I must say that the interest I take in the Society*[4] is entirely dependent on the decision in reference to this point. The edition of the *Anthems* was so unsatisfactory, on account of the new marking, that I would never use it for the purposes of a public performance. I wish to know, above all things, what is Handel's and what is not. This desire the Council shared with me last year; but now the opposite views seem to prevail, and if they are adopted, I for one (and a *good many* with me, I believe) will much prefer the old edition, with its incorrect notes, to the new one with its various conceptions and performance indications. All that, I have written to Macfarren. You aren't angry with me for speaking out so plainly, are you? My opinion is so intimately connected with what I have held to be right, all my life, that I could not possibly alter it.[5]

Let me also cite the following passages from a letter by Brahms to Rudorff (dated November 1, 1877): "I would like to be as generous here (in the critical commentary) as I am sparing there (in the music itself!)." And later: "In the *A*-minor Ballade I would also leave the [six quarter notes under a triplet sign] although they seem inexplicable to me. The same applies to this *A* which, besides, does show some correspondence with this later passage." (Musical examples are given.) "The three fifths definitely must remain!" (A musical example follows.) Finally: "I wish very much that Bargiel would agree with us in not attempting to improve on Chopin's orthography! From here it would be only a small step to attack his texture as well."[6]

I have thus marshalled evidence and allowed the masters to speak for themselves. Those who are not convinced are welcome to continue to put their trust in such men as Bülow and Reinecke; it is obvious that even in matters of art, they are simply at the mercy of blind faith!

May this study help us realize that such masters as J. S. Bach, C.P.E. Bach, Haydn, Mozart, Beethoven, and Chopin possess musical intellects of an innately superior order, intellects that transcend, to an infinite degree, the wisdom of their editors.

Commentary

1. THE CHROMATIC FANTASY

J. S. Bach wrote only a few fantasias; their form, while it tended to differ from work to work, was always well defined. Later, C.P.E. Bach, Mozart, and Beethoven often used a certain basic plan to great advantage: they wrote fantasias in which short, homophonic segments—self-contained and nicely rounded off—alternated with transitional passage work or preludizing material.[*7] It is curious that J. S. Bach made more use of this form in his toccatas,[*8] though it would have been a natural choice for his fantasias. Of course, the practice of the time demanded that the homophonic sections be replaced with wholly polyphonic pieces written in a strict or free fugal style; these provided optimal contrast to the transitional passages or recitative sections.

The Chromatic Fantasy itself has a highly individual form: it consists of two parts, both having the same length and carrying the same weight. The first (bars 1-49) is a true prelude while the second (bars 49-79) is written in the style of a recitative.

Since the inherent characteristics of passage work and recitative writing could lure a composer into using tonal procedures that are both aimless and irrational, Bach's artistry in finding the most felicitous solution to this double problem is awesome indeed. Consider this: within the 49 bars of the first part, he arrives upon V of the main tonality no fewer than seven times (in bars 4, 6, 8, 29, 30, 41, and 49)! On the one hand this creates sectionality, leading to heightened clarity of design—each V can almost be considered a divider![9] On the other hand, because of the persistent circling around the dominant, the feeling of the main tonality is never lost. What sureness of instinct to use such simple means to maintain the key amidst tumultuous runs, passages, and arpeggios! The treatment of tonality in the recitative is even more interesting. The dominant is followed by a few brief motions away from the main key, proceeding by thirds with chromatic alterations (bars 50-62). But, beginning in bar 62, the main tonality establishes itself so firmly that there can be absolutely no doubt about its identity. V (A) is heard in bar 62; I, with a chromatically altered third (F♯), follows in bar 63; the tonic degree is retained until bar 68 (!), when IV appears. Then, in bar 70, there is a regular half cadence, and finally, in bar 74, an equally regular full cadence. Could any motion be more tonal? And yet, what an achievement in a work that seems (but only *seems*) to be entirely chromatic and even atonal! Unfortunately, Spitta failed to notice this important feature of Bach's technique; in his biography of the composer, he characterizes this work as "all uncontrolled 'storm and stress'" and writes:

> This celebrated work must have been written, at the latest, in 1730, and internal evidence convinces us that it must be assigned to a considerably earlier date; the Fantasy bears a perceptible resemblance to the piece of the same name which precedes the great Organ Fugue in *G* minor. This was written before 1725, and we found reason for connecting it with Bach's journey to Hamburg in 1720. Thus it is quite possible, and even probable, when we take into consideration another and an older form of the work which still exists, that the Chromatic Fantasy and Fugue may also date from before the Leipzig period. The effervescent character which pervades both pieces is not in the spirit of the Leipzig productions; and, even in his fantasias, Bach is not wont to dispense with strict forms, developed either thematically or episodically [*motivisch oder thematisch*]. Here all is uncontrolled "storm and stress." The bold idea of transplanting the recitative into a keyboard piece had already been embodied in Bach's earlier Fantasy in *D* major; its germ is found in the works of the northern organists, and its development was assisted by Bach's intimacy with Vivaldi's violin concertos. In the Chromatic Fantasy this idea attained a grand perfection. The piece, in which the boldest feats of modulation are crowded together, has the effect of an emotional *scena*. The Fugue worthily carries out the chromatic character and the startling modulations of the piece, and the treatment of the Fugue is full of genius, with a mighty demoniacal rush.[*10]

Bar 2

The sixteenth rest at the beginning of bar 2 is missing in the Bülow, Peters, and Reinecke editions. This arbitrary omission by the editors arises from a widespread and dangerous misconception. Instead of choosing a tempo that would allow an accurate realization of Bach's original succession of thirty-second and sixty-fourth notes, here (and in many other passages) a preconceived, rigidly immutable tempo is adopted, a tempo so fast that it permits no differentiation of note values in performance. Unaware that the error lies in his tempo, an editor is easily misled into making a disfiguring change: as a natural consequence of his style of playing, he eliminates Bach's sixteenth rest and simply transforms the sixty-fourth notes, which he is unable to perform as such, into thirty-second notes. The resultant uniformity of the durational values is then improperly attributed to Bach himself![*11]

There is no valid reason for changing the $b\natural^1$ occurring within the second quarter to a $b\flat^1$, as Bülow does. However, either would be correct at this point.

Bar 3

A different version of bars 3-20 is found in the so-called Rust manuscript.[*12] The relevance of this source has unfortunately never been—and perhaps can never be—clarified. This much is certain: since the Rust version shows a complete lack of variety in its figures, it must—from a purely artistic and technical point of view—be ranked far below the version that appears in the other manuscripts (on which I base my edition). It seems likely that Bach himself progressed from an earlier, rather stiff and monotonous version to a later setting showing greater freedom and diversity—much as Beethoven (though in a broader framework and style) progressed from the Leonore Overture no. 2 to the technical improvements of Overture no. 3. It is hardly likely that the copyist preparing the Rust manuscript, faced with the beautifully finished version, would have wished to try out some inferior motivic writing of his own. Yet the lack of insight shown by so many writers and editors knows no bounds!

Bar 4

This bar could have begun with a literal repetition of at least the first half of bar 3; instead the figure appears with a small alteration. This change, however modest, serves as the first demonstration within the scope of the present work of Bach's practical commitment to the artistic *principle of variety*. For this point marks the divergence of the Rust version (if indeed it may be considered Bach's own work) and the later setting. Without the initial contrast that the later setting provides—and the recognition of its significance as a compositional factor is very important!—Bach would have consigned himself to the monotony of the Rust version. Instead, by introducing contrast as a driving force, he pledged himself to variety. Indeed, we shall find that every note of this marvelous work will preach the grand sermon of variety! C.P.E. Bach says it so beautifully in his *Versuch über die wahre Art das Clavier zu spielen*, in the chapter entitled "The Free Fantasia":

> The beauty of variety is made evident in the fantasia. A diversified figuration and all attributes of good performance must be employed. The ear tires of unrelieved passage work, sustained chords, or broken chords. By themselves they neither stir nor still the passions; and it is for these purposes that the fantasia is exceptionally well suited. Broken chords must not progress too rapidly or unevenly. Occasional exceptions to this precept may be introduced with good effect into chromatic progressions. The performer must not break his chords constantly in a single color. . . . Those who are capable will do well when they depart from a too natural use of harmony to introduce an occasional deception; but if their attainments are insufficient for the purpose, they must enhance by means of a varied and fine execution of all manner of figuration those harmonies which sound plain when performed in the usual style. . . . [*13]

Bar 5

In the fourth quarter of this measure, the question of whether the second sixteenth of the first eighth should be read as bb^1 or $b\natural^1$ must be decided in favor of bb^1.[14] The sketch of the underlying harmonies given in example 1 shows that the lower voice moves down in quarter notes from d^2 through c^2-bb^1: d^2-c^2-bb^1-$a^1 | g^1$, while the upper voice moves down from f^2, also in quarter notes, through $c\sharp^2$-bb^1: f^2-e^2-d^2-$c\sharp^2 | bb^1$.

Example 1

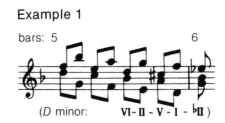

bars: 5   6

(*D* minor: VI - II - V - I - $\flat$II)

In the piece itself the thirds formed between these two voices are composed out,[15] causing the augmented second bb^1-$c\sharp^2$ to appear on the third quarter of the measure as part of the sixteenth-note succession bb^1-$c\sharp^2$-d^2. Since bb^1 is also heard in the first quarter of the next measure (bar 6), linear considerations alone make $b\natural^1$ unthinkable in the fourth quarter of bar 5, precisely between the two bb^1s (bar 5, third quarter; bar 6, first quarter)! Therefore the $b\natural^1$ given by Bülow and Reinecke must be considered incorrect.

Bar 7

One must understand the voice leading in this measure (shown in example 2) in order to avoid Busoni's curious mistake in the second quarter of the bar where, on the fifth sixteenth, he calls for emphasis of the $b\natural^1$ in performance. (A similar situation exists in bar 9.)[16]

Example 2

bar 7

In the third quarter of this measure, however, there is the question of whether the second sixteenth should be read as $e\flat^1$ or, according to Bülow's assumption, as $e\natural^1$, with $e\flat^1$ withheld until the fifth sixteenth. The answer to this question rests on the principle of elision—and not on "authenticity" or "inauthenticity" as Bischoff would have it.[17] Application of this principle obviates the need for proceeding to the chromatic $e\flat^1$ by way of the diatonic $e\natural^1$; one may immediately sound the chromatic tone $e\flat^1$ (instead of $e\natural^1$).

Bar 10

The harmonies change more rapidly (see example 3) than in the foregoing bars 7-9; this acceleration must be expressed in performance.

Example 3
bars: 10   11

Bar 11

In the last quarter of this measure, the Reinecke edition has c instead of d in the right-hand part, at the second sixteenth (see example 4).

Example 4

Regrettably, Reinecke's alteration is also condoned by the Bach-Gesellschaft edition, not in the score itself, but most definitively in the preface, where it is characterized as follows: "a very plausible reading that logically retains the interval of a fourth; however, the manuscripts all have d rather than c."[*18] Thus there is a double necessity to refute this correction. The basis for Reinecke's version, as is correctly stated in the above citation, is the purely external requirement of "logically" retaining the fourth—and it was assumed that this was important to Bach. Not so! The reasons for Bach's instinctive choice of d are far deeper and more meaningful than Reinecke could have suspected. First, the $^6_4$ position A-d-f found here is intended as a response to the $^6_4$ position d-g-$b\flat$ found in the third quarter of the preceding bar; second—and this is the important reason!—Bach specifically chose d so that we might hear the tonic harmony with renewed emphasis, just as he ensured our perception of the subdominant in the preceding bar! So profound, and at the same time so simple: by illuminating IV and I in bars 10 and 11, more light is shed on all the chromatic activity that surrounds them! We will observe a similar situation in bar 75, where we will have even greater cause to marvel at the wisdom and beauty of Bach's instincts, which arise from such immeasurable depths.

Bar 12

How wonderfully surprising is the harmony C-$E\flat$-G in the first half of the measure! But once a complete chromatic change has taken place, at the appearance of VII or V of the main tonality (D minor), it is as if the initial harmony had simply been a free suspension (*einen freien Vorhalt*), as shown in example 5.[*19]

Example 5

bars: 12   13

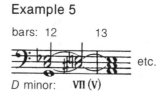

etc.

D minor: VII (V)

Bar 16

While the sixteenth notes f^1-g^1-a^1 are heard in the first quarter of the measure (at the second eighth), one should note that the succession f^1-$g\sharp^1$-a^1 is heard in both the second and fourth quarters.[20]

Bar 17

The chord built on the chromatically raised IV, $G\sharp$-$B\natural$-D-F,[*21] which is composed out here, takes on the character of VII in A minor; this is compatible with the use of $c\natural^2$ in the second quarter of the measure. Immediately thereafter, however, at the fourth quarter, one finds that this chord, its existing character still intact, shows the influence of the succeeding chord; it is the proximity of the approaching V of the next measure that gives rise to the use of $c\sharp^1$ rather than $c\natural^1$. What unusual delicacy of instinct is shown in this use of $c\sharp^1$ as if to provide a foretaste of the approaching flavor—to bridge the transition to the next chord! What benefits the technique of composing-out provides!

Bar 18

Example 6 summarizes the contents of this measure. A cursory examination might yield the interpretation given in example 7, which indeed would be what most composers, lacking sufficient technique, would write in such situations.

Example 6   Example 7

Example 6 shows that Bach has composed out a two-voice passing motion within the dominant. The root as well as the seventh of the dominant chord are sustained; however, the effect of the sustained seventh could be achieved only by writing d^1-$b\flat$, a leap of a third, rather than d^1-c^1, a step of a second, in the third quarter of the measure. This leap allows the seventh, g, to be reached on the first sixteenth note of the fourth quarter. The inimitable artistry with which passing sonorities are composed out—so unique and distinctive to Bach—is manifest here![*22]

Bar 19

This measure reveals another unique feature of Bach's style—the incomparable virtuosity of his treatment of rhythm. A figure consisting of five notes, repeated several times, is incorporated into a $\frac{4}{4}$ meter whose quarter notes each comprise six sixteenth notes! How especially arresting are the frictions and conflicts that arise: the accents of the $\frac{4}{4}$ meter and especially those of the six sixteenth notes, oppose those of the five-note figure! Note the special effect of this rhythmic technique: when the five-note figure first appears in the first quarter of the measure, it begins on the second sixteenth; at each subsequent repetition the figure of necessity begins one sixteenth sooner, that is, on the first, sixth, fifth, and fourth sixteenths of the second, third, and fourth quarters respectively. It is as though each repetition were motivated by the initial tone's desire to reach a strong, or even relatively strong part of the measure; thus, when the beginning of the motive finally does coincide with the relatively strong fourth sixteenth (i.e., at the second eighth of the fourth quarter), this arrival automatically extinguishes any further propulsive power. If one examines the rhythmic locations at which the motive begins, i.e., the sixteenth-note positions indicated above: (3), 2, 1, 6, 5, 4, ‖ (3),[23] one might imagine that this series opens, inscribes, and closes a mysterious, mystical circle![*24]

The Bülow, Peters, and Reinecke editions unfortunately assume that $c\sharp^2$ in the third quarter of the bar is followed by $b\flat^1$ rather than $b\natural^1$ (on the second sixteenth note). However, I believe that $b\natural^1$ should already be heard at this point in the bar, for the following reasons. In the approach to $c\sharp^2$ (which falls on the second sixteenth note of the first quarter of bar 20), the major (raised) sixth, $b\natural^1$, serves as a better passing tone than the diatonic minor sixth, $b\flat^1$ (on the fourth quarter of bar 19). But this single $b\natural^1$, so close to the end of the measure, is not strong enough to establish the hidden line ($b\natural^1$-$c\sharp^2$) effectively; for this express purpose Bach requires the assistance of an earlier, additional $b\natural^1$ (replacing $b\flat^1$)—the one under discussion here.[*25]

The penultimate sixteenth note must be read as f^2, and not as $f\#^2$, as Bischoff, Busoni, and Röntgen have it. One should be aware of the compositional reason, so characteristic of Bach's artistry. The $g\#^2$ that occurs on the second eighth of the fourth quarter enters as the initial tone of the last repetition of the five-note figure. In this position, it automatically and without detriment to its passing role suggests a chord of the raised IV in D minor, $g\#$-$b\natural$-d-f. While composing out a harmony over longer stretches, Bach particularly liked to introduce a hidden suggestion of such individual chords that arise from passing motion, especially when, as here, the occasion is so fleeting. Thus f^2 together with $g\#^2$ and d^2 sound like a partial expression (*Teilharmonie*) of precisely this kind of passing chord.[*26]

Bar 20

Several editions (e.g., Reinecke, Bischoff) offer different readings for the last eighth note, a^2, and its short trill (*Pralltriller*).[27] One variant is given in example 8.[28]

Example 8

While it may be true that the editor or performer, in accordance with the traditional rules governing the fermata,[*29] has every right to exercise license in precisely this kind of passage, Bülow's version, which goes far beyond the reading given in example 8, must be regarded as an abuse of this license.[30] My personal choice here would be an abrupt short trill, which cuts into the flow of the music so suddenly and decisively. Moreover, the short trill provides the most effective foil for the thirty-second rest that opens the next measure.

Bar 21

The variety evident in the rhythmic placement of the chord tones $b\flat^2$-g^2-e^2 (bar 21) as well as $b\flat^1$-g^1-e^1 and $b\flat$-g-e (bar 22)[*31] shows the vast superiority of the reading given in the score over that found in a second extant version (see example 9).[*32]

Example 9: Variant reading of bars 21-24

Bar 25

In the second quarter, the third note from the end must definitely be read as $f\sharp^1$, not as $f\natural^1$, the unfortunate reading found in most editions (Bach-Gesellschaft, Peters, Bischoff, Busoni, etc.).[33] The choice of $F\sharp$ (rather than $F\natural$) may be explained as follows: If we direct our attention to the three-note figures beginning with $g\sharp$ and $b\natural$—the first two components of the composed-out chord $G\sharp$-$B\natural$-D-F—we perceive their sum as the triad E-$G\sharp$-$B\natural$ (see example 10).

Example 10

However, the figures beginning with d^1 and f^1—the last two components of the composed-out chord—express the diminished triad $B\natural$-D-F (see example 11).

Example 11

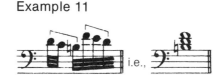

Now, we are familiar with Bach's customary procedure in composing out such chordal fragments (*Teilharmonien*).[*34] In this instance, each time the first two components are set in motion, a reading of $F\sharp$ becomes mandatory, for the sake of the momentary appearance of the chord E-$G\sharp$-$B\natural$; it is almost as though this chord were to express I in E major.

Bar 27

This measure brings us to an extremely important subject, namely, the question of the *arpeggio*.

It is high time one realized that the traditional written and oral directives for the performance of arpeggios provide instruction in what is basically the most elementary technique. I speak here of the rules governing the arpeggiation of chords of longer duration—which originally called for a single ascent and descent, then later prescribed double or multiple ascending and descending arpeggios—as well as the arpeggiation of chords of shorter duration with a single ascending or descending arpeggio. This minimal technique, whether learned from textbooks or in private study, could be expected of everyone in every period. However, it is a sad mistake to believe that this achievement of lesser talents represents the technique's ultimate perfection, and that it also can, or indeed must, satisfy the most demanding artistic obligations at the highest levels.[*35] A study of the arpeggio technique of J. S. Bach or C.P.E. Bach, as seen in their own written-out arpeggiations, will convincingly show that these composers aimed for the highest artistic standards of beauty and perfection in the voice leading of their arpeggiated passages!*[36] An example will help clarify these observations.[37]

Let us imagine that, close to the end of J. S. Bach's Prelude and Fugue in A minor,*[38] the composer, instead of writing out his own arpeggiation, had merely supplied the performer with chords (perhaps as in example 12).*[39]

Example 12

What would the performer play then? Nothing but two ascending and descending arpeggios, as the "rule" dictates.

But now let us enter a different sphere, the glorious world created by Bach (see example 13).

Example 13: J. S. Bach, Prelude in A Minor, bars 77-85 (with Schenker's annotations)

Above all, note how Bach exploits the close position of his chords. Instead of limiting his arpeggiation to chord tones (*harmonische Töne*), he interpolates regular diatonic passing tones and acciaccaturas.[40] Undoubtedly, these little dissonant notes have an enlivening effect and thus enhance the beauty of the passage. In addition, he gives his arpeggio figure a very characteristic angular profile: just before changing from an upward to a downward direction, he suddenly bends back (see the last two thirty-second notes of the third quarter of the first figure). Thus, after laying down some basic specifications applicable in this particular case, Bach commences his arpeggiation. What miracles of voice leading await us in the details!

At the second arpeggiation of the first figure, Bach abruptly eliminates the $g\sharp^1$ from his descent; this enables him to use the lower $g\sharp$ as his final note. But to what purpose? Obviously to avoid the juxtaposition of two a's, which would have created a kind of musical hiatus, and which would have been unavoidable if the figure had remained unchanged in its second descent. How beautifully does the step of a second, $g\sharp$-a, now lead into the second figure!

At the second figure, note how $g\sharp^1$ (the seventh thirty-second note of the ascent) leads into a^1 which, however, is delayed until the second thirty-second note of the descent. We see here the tension generated by an interrupted passing tone or, if you will, an acciaccatura.

At the beginning of the third figure, Bach avoids the non-diatonic succession (see example 14) which would have resulted if he had adhered to his original specifications.

Example 14

etc.

Instead, he substitutes the angular version shown in example 15.

Example 15

etc.

For the same reason he ends the figure with another similarly angular succession. What estimable attention to detail!

Warranting even higher praise is the manifestation of Bach's instincts in the transition from the fourth to the fifth figure. He is reluctant to write a simple repetition of the first arpeggiation (see example 16), not only because he needs to express the $^6_4$ chord, but also because, after so much stepwise motion, the skip of a third from a weak to a strong part of the measure would produce a poor effect.[*41] Therefore, he ends his arpeggiated figure with d^1 rather than b, which additionally results in a powerful descending fifth, much more effective than a third.

Example 16

etc.

A similar desire for a powerful bass motion causes Bach to use another fifth at the end of the fifth figure instead of the step of a second that would certainly have been possible (see example 17).

Example 17

But the profundity of Bach's technique is most apparent in the concluding passages of the last three figures. In the score, instead of the endings for the seventh, eighth, and ninth figures shown in example 18 (I give only the last four notes of each arpeggiation), every final group descends from *b*, a pattern established in the fifth figure.

Example 18

What does this signify? This impressive voice leading may be explained as follows: Since *b* could be used as the uniform initial tone of the last thirty-second-note group in the fifth, sixth, eighth, and ninth figures, Bach did not wish to make an exception for the intervening seventh figure; he did not wish to disturb the series of successive *b*'s with an *a*! (The *a* would otherwise have been a better choice.) Consequently, the *b* in the seventh figure is a substitute for the chord tone *a*, and thus assumes the role of an accented passing tone (*Wechselnote*).[42]

Moreover, the reason for the use of *a* instead of *f♯* for the last note of the arpeggiation in the seventh figure is related to the explanation given above in my discussion of the fourth and fifth figures. Here too, we see the avoidance of an abrupt skip of a third after a series of seconds when moving to a strong part of the measure.

The roles assumed by the last four notes in the ninth figure are indicated in example 19.[*43]

Example 19

What consummate artistic wisdom, what power is seen in this attentiveness to every tone, even those that seem the most insignificant! Each is given its own entirely fitting and appropriate part to play within the whole.

And now, when this unparalleled artist leaves the execution of an arpeggio to the performer, he is insolently offered a childish technique, one that shows not the slightest trace of artistic infusion! Time and again one encounters the same kind of performance: the chord tones or other notes indicated in the figure are played as an ascending and descending arpeggio whose peak is always placed on the strong part of the measure. In a particularly inspired mood one might venture to add a note in the lower octave *ad pompam ed ostentationem!*

An examination of the realizations given for the arpeggiated passages in the various editions of the Chromatic Fantasy will substantiate my complaint. I will thus attempt, to the best of my meager ability, a realization that aims for higher standards—and anyone is welcome to suggest a different and better version. My suggested realization of bars 27-29 takes Bach's own beginning as a point of departure, continuing the same kind of triplet arpeggio for each succeeding chord (see example 20).

Example 20

for bars 27-29

Bar 33

The second arpeggiated passage begins in this bar; its first chord follows quite logically from the chord in bar 30, bridging bars 31-32, in which that chord is composed out. This skillful and extremely important artistic technique of creating harmonic connections even across interpolated passages is one of the hidden features of Bach's consummate writing. We blithely enjoy it without, however, being able to account for it. For purposes of comparison I present two further examples, both from the Organ Toccata in *D* minor (in Tausig's arrangement; see example 21).

Example 21: J. S. Bach, Organ Toccata in D Minor (Tausig)

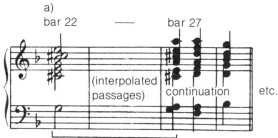

35

b) before the end:

Such connections should unquestionably be expressed in performance, but this is possible only if the performer has a highly developed harmonic imagination and can sense along with the composer, as it were, the future course of the harmony beyond the interpolations.[44]

As for the arpeggiation that begins in bar 33, the realization I suggest in example 22 contrasts with those given in other editions.

Example 22

for bars 33-41

A full awareness of the meaning of the harmonic motion in the arpeggiated passage is essential (see example 23).[*45]

Example 23

bars: 33 — 34 — 35 — 36 — 38 — 39 — 40 — 41 — 42

D — B♮ — E — A — F — D — E♭ — A — B♭

i.e., D minor: I#3 ♮VI#3 II#3 V#3 III♭7 I♮3-#3 ♭II V#3 VI

A critical comparison of other versions with the chords as given and notated in my score—in this case, I give the same chords as the Bach-Gesellschaft edition—is beyond the scope of this study, though it certainly would have been profitable, from a compositional point of view, to have detailed the reasons for my choice.

Bar 49

This measure marks the beginning of the *recitative*, which gives rise to the following observations.

The harmonic motion governing bars 49-70 is outlined in example 24.[46]

Example 24

bars: 49   —   50 — 55   —   56   57   —   58 — 60   —   61   62 — 63 — 68

A – D#3 — F – G♭♭7 — E♭ – F♭(E) — C♯ – B♯ — G♯ – C♯   A♮7 – D – G
                                major

D minor: V - I   B♭ minor: V - VI   A♭ minor: V - ♭VI   F♯ minor: V - #IV   C♯ minor: VII-V - I   D minor: V#3 - I#3-IV

motion by a third   motion by a third   motion by a third   motion by a third
with chromatic   with chromatic   with chromatic   with chromatic
alteration   alteration   alteration   alteration

— 69 — 70
— C♯ — D-G-A   etc.
♯VII — I-IV-V

But of far greater interest is the concealed, deeply embedded melodic line that courses through almost the entire recitative, beginning at $b\flat^1$ and descending chromatically through an octave! This line may be read most easily at the eighth notes sounding with those chords that—in the form of passionate outbursts—serve both as the starting points and the goals of the individual recitative statements. May this hidden compositional miracle fill us with wonder and delight (see example 25).*[47]

Example 25

bars: 49-54   56   59 or 61   63   67

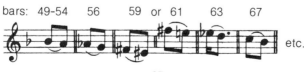

etc.

What discipline is evident here, a discipline of doubled merit in the context of a recitative, where a composer could so easily yield to the lure of undisciplined freedom! Now we know the inner source of the unique power that Bach's music does, and indeed must, exert!

It is self-evident that the contents of a recitative should be performed with the greatest possible freedom, and that the bar lines should merely assist in realizing the general outlines of the ideas. Yet even the most boundless freedom should be secretly governed by the constraints of meter. In other words, freedom in performance should never cause the listener to imagine different note values from those indicated by the actual original rhythmic organization of the measure.

One of the most reprehensible liberties taken in performance is that of abbreviating the first note of every recitative statement. In many editions, unfortunately, this is reflected in the notation of the initial tone, which is given a shorter duration (see example 26).[*48]

Example 26

However sincerely an editor may desire that this type of notation not be misinterpreted by the performer,[*49] I still regard it as dangerous that a performer should even be permitted to set eyes on it! For I believe that it is not always advisable to commit to notation the liberties taken in performance, impelled by fleeting perceptions. In the face of such subtlety, does not the notation always say either too much or too little?

One may of course arpeggiate all of the chords that appear in the recitative.

Bar 50

With this bar we come to one of the most controversial questions posed by the text. Several editions, among them the Busoni, Röntgen, and even the Bach-Gesellschaft editions, replace the chord *Gb-A-C-Eb* with *Gb-Ab*(!)-*C-Eb*. They then alter the subsequent notes so that they conform to the chord (see example 27).[*50]

Example 27

bar 50

etc.

Yet if one recalls my discussion of bar 49 regarding the harmonic motion and especially regarding the concealed line, one reaches the obvious conclusion that the succession bb^1-a^1 constitutes the only possible reading for the second quarter of the measure, and that these notes can pertain only to the chord *A-C-Eb-Gb*, VII in *Bb* major/minor. Bach proceeds as follows: After stating the chord *A-C♯-E* in bar 49, he moves to *D-F♯-A* on the fourth quarter of that measure; he retains this same chord during the first half of bar 50, only he extends it to the ninth, *eb*, so that it includes the outer limit of the VII chord.[51] The resultant sum is thus *(D)-F♯-A-C-Eb*.[*52] At this point, however, Bach conceives the plan of moving up by a third from the *D* chord to the *F* chord, to which he will assign the role of V in *Bb* major/minor. In order to obtain this objective, he wisely decides to give the performer adequate visual preparation for what is to come: he enharmonically renotates the first chord, *F♯-A-C-Eb*, as *Gb-A-C-Eb* (!). Nothing could be simpler. However, most editors fail to see this connection; in dealing with manuscript or text they simply overlook and misunderstand the enharmonic change—*Gb* is taken at its face value, and is related in a superficially correct way to the *Db*-major chord.[*53] As a result of this error, the succeeding notes are unhesitatingly derived from V in *Db* major (as shown in example 27), rather than from V in *Bb* major. But what a terrible effect this creates! Bach may of course be credited with the most daring harmonic successions, but they are never illogical! As an example, one may recall the surprising and daring harmonic motion in the *G*-minor Prelude and Fugue for organ (bar 14 ff.)[*54] where VII in *D* minor, respelled enharmonically, continues on as VII in *B* minor; it then proceeds via a descending third, *B-G*, to *C* minor. *C* minor surely could have been reached from *D* minor by a more direct and natural route than by an enharmonic detour through *B* minor, a distant key using sharps. And yet a logical basis in *B* minor may be found at least for the point of departure, the VII chord in *D* minor. But in our present example, how are we to give a logical explanation for the reading of *Ab* in bar 50? Can we really believe that Bach would have wished the abrupt succession from *D-F♯-A* to *Ab-C-Eb-(Gb)*? What would be its significance or purpose? Or might one perhaps stretch the definition of the term "fantasia" so far as to justify even this grotesque succession? In my opinion, however, this crude and sudden harmonic jolt would be inconsistent with Bach's desire, in our Fantasy, to be bound by the strict discipline of a truly profound and hidden controlling force!

Bar 62

The trill appears with its suffix ($f♯^2$) and an anticipation (a^2, which belongs to the next chord).[*55] Since the suffix does not appear in its simplest and purest form, a very small separation should occur between the last note of the trill and the $f♯^2$.[*56] The alternate execution shown in example 28 is permitted only if one employs a fairly long trill. In that case the trill proceeds without interruption; it moves directly to the suffix $f♯^2$, which leads to the last two notes.[57]

Example 28

Bar 65

Observe Bach's virtuosity as he incorporates into the $\frac{4}{4}$ meter a motive—repeated several times—composed basically of ten thirty-second notes.

Bar 67

A trill with a suffix could be performed here (see example 29).[58]

Example 29

Bar 75

After completing his cadence, Bach constructs a final organ point at the tonic. Example 30 presents a sketch of the chords heard over this organ point.

Example 30

We find a chain of diminished seventh chords, descending by half steps. At first glance, it might seem quite unusual that in just three places in this descent there is a sudden interruption by a simple triad. These triads are the same ones referred to in my discussion of bar 11 above,[59] namely those on IV, I, and again on IV; they are finally brought to a conclusion at the V–I progression in the last bars! I ask, what other composer would show such attentiveness? While moving through so many diminished seventh chords, who else would give any thought to IV and I and their need for expression as pure, serene, and complete triads?! Let us kneel in devotion before Bach's majestic spirit!

Instead of playing the original figures found in my edition, it has become traditional to substitute variant readings, such as those given in example 31.[*60]

Of course, this kind of passage lends itself to the performance of "elaborate embellishments"(*weitläufigere Manieren*)—to use an expression of C.P.E. Bach's;[*61]

Example 31: Variant reading of bars 76–79

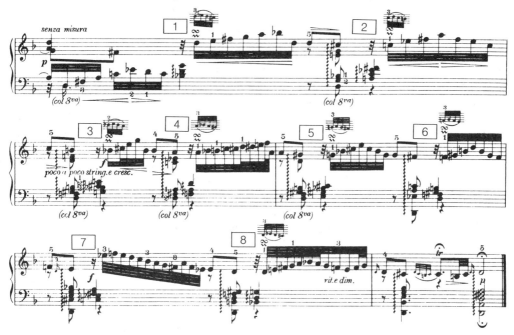

yet these should at least meet the requirements of good taste. Unfortunately, this is by no means true of the variants cited in the example.

But if the reader is to understand my criticism, he must allow me to expound the merits of Bach's original figures. They are based on the sixteenth-note arpeggiations shown in example 32.

Example 32

As one can see, there are five ascending arpeggiations; at the sixth, in order to introduce contrast and variety—oh! what a blessing are these principles!—the type of arpeggiation is changed, and this alteration prevails for the last three arpeggiations (bars 77–78).

Now to Bach's compositional elaboration (*Ausführung*). He lays his bearings with the simplest sixteenth-note form, the same as that shown at the beginning of my schematic representation. The second figure is more active; the third (bar 76) is closer to the first. It is followed by the fourth figure, which shows more similarity to the second (though the initial tone is shortened). The fifth figure (bar 77), unrolling enriched figuration, is different again, and so on until the eighth and final figure (bar 78), assisted by sixty-fourth notes, unfolds the richest elaboration. What refined and delicate balance is created by this contrast and variety; the notes are so beautifully distributed in regard to quantity alone![62]

By contrast, when we turn to the variant readings, we already find needless complexity and excessive agitation in the first figure! In this form, how can it logically serve as a standard for the construction of the succeeding figures? Surely confusion and disorder will reign if the foundation itself is not concise. What kind of effect can be produced by the sudden simplicity of the third figure, coming as it does after the complexities of the first two figures? And then the fourth figure enters forthwith as an embellishment whose gaudiness and richness serve as a direct rebuff to the simplicity of the third figure! Furthermore, how can one justify the fact that the composer of these variants continues to arpeggiate the sixth figure in the same ascending direction as the first five, in disregard of the wonderful sense of contrast evident in Bach's version?! How meager was his competence to emulate Bach's taste! Last and worst of all, in bar 78, after all this excess, Bach's original eighth and final figure is retained. I ask, can this be tolerated? Bach gave it the most careful preparation, increasing the intensity and richness so that it appeared to be the best and most enduring version—how can it possibly be used here in the company of the other variants, when the same richness is already evident in the fourth figure and is even present in the closely adjacent seventh figure? Is this economy? Is this artistry? How can such uneconomical writing be effective? Does this all fall under the heading of understanding and serving Bach? Whoever is responsible for these variants, whether (as is believed) it be Bach's own sons or Forkel,[63] and whoever promulgates them (Bülow, for example) gives absolutely no evidence of refined taste and shows no understanding for high compositional art! What then can be expected of those who are still in need of guidance if their so-called guides themselves possess so little insight into art!

2. THE FUGUE

All of the entrances of the fugal theme are given in table I; this tabulation will help us gain an understanding of the fugue's large-scale construction.

TABLE I

The first section, the exposition, comprises the first three entrances, as follows: subject—answer—subject (*D* minor—*A* minor—*D* minor). It ends with a cadence leading to *F* major (bar 35). Bars 35-41 of the episode are followed by the second section.

The second section begins with the fourth and fifth entrances (subject—subject), still in *A* minor and *D* minor, but the succeeding entrances, the sixth and seventh (answer—subject), are in distant keys, namely *B* minor and *E* minor. This is in

43

keeping with the basic function of the middle section of a fugue as the modulatory section. Whether the next two entrances, the eighth and ninth (*D* minor, *G* minor) should be assigned to the second or third section is open to question. I prefer to assume that the third section begins with the eighth entrance; therefore bar 106 marks the end of the second section.

Thus the third section encompasses the eighth through eleventh entrances. My reason for considering these four entrances as a unit lies in the relationship of their keys. The fact that the ninth entrance brings with it the key of the subdominant, *G* minor, suggests to me that it seeks to establish itself as a midpoint between the eighth and tenth entrances (both in *D* minor)—a midpoint whose purpose it is to be surmounted for cadential reasons.[64] For it is much more appropriate that the subdominant be included as an essential element of the cadence. Once the subdominant force of the ninth entrance has been overcome, the conclusive power of the tenth and eleventh entrances becomes all the greater. In addition, one should note that the tenth entrance follows the ninth almost immediately; there is only the briefest of episodes between them!*[65]

N.B. In table I, the brackets appearing within the individual entrances indicate those places or measures in which a change has been made in the fugal theme; these changes will be discussed in detail in the ensuing commentary. The entrances themselves, the so-called "voices" of the fugue, should be conceived only as actual instrumental parts, as true keyboard lines; one ought never equate them with genuine vocal types such as soprano, alto, tenor, or bass. I wish to establish this point firmly in advance because almost all editors of instrumental fugues, as well as theorists—in analyses given in editions (that may or may not be printed in various colors!),[66] books, or instruction manuals—are misled time and again by the admittedly tempting association of instrumental lines and vocal types. Failing to recognize the purely instrumental character of the setting, such writers carry on endlessly about "soprano," "alto," "tenor," and "bass," endowing these terms with a meaning that is more than merely associative! They have still not grasped the difference between the voices of a vocal fugue and those of an instrumental fugue. At best, they manage to show tolerance for an instrumental "voice" when it exceeds the range of its corresponding vocal type. But no! Instrumental lines and vocal types are fundamentally different. Analogies with vocal types should not be permitted to cloud the artistic perception of those having a genuine desire to understand instrumental fugal technique—especially that of J. S. Bach. In this commentary, then, I will refer to the voices of this Fugue simply as upper, middle, and lower, or first (= upper), second (= middle), and third (= lower).

Bar 1

The subject appears in the upper voice (bars 1-8).

If we take the first quarter note of bar 1 and add on to this a^1 the first quarter notes of bars 4, 6, 7, and 8, the succession shown in example 33 will result.

Example 33

Thus the veil is lifted from a wondrous and profound mystery. All of the chromaticism of the subject, seemingly so diffuse and aimless, is in fact firmly rooted in the composed-out *D*-minor chord. Indeed, it is as if we heard only the composed-out chord itself! What inspired construction!!*[67]

One should note the following feature of the subject: Written in *D* minor, it begins on the dominant, in order that it may close on the tonic (bar 8).

Bar 8

Aside from the opening d^1, this bar is no longer part of the fugal theme. It is an insertion, whose presence is obligatory for technical reasons. First among these is the fact that the subject ends on the tonic (d^1); this makes it difficult for the answer to enter immediately, for it must begin with the same d^1 (see bar 9). Second, the upper voice, after stating the subject, must continue with the first countersubject. It must therefore rise considerably higher than the answer's middle-voice entrance in order to avoid a beginning under the answer or a voice crossing, both of which would be incompatible with its new role as the upper counterpoint. These important reasons would have sufficed to justify the insertion of bar 8. Bach, however, took the added precaution of eradicating all signs of technical awkwardness for, as is well known, such insertions are often to be criticized, especially if they betray a momentary perplexity after the completion of the subject (common among lesser composers). Bach's solution is worthy of his genius; he conceived the idea of using the motive of the inserted bar as the nucleus of the first countersubject (see bar 10 and the inversion of this motive in bars 12 and 15). Thus the insertion, which undoubtedly arose out of technical necessity, came to be endowed with a genuinely inspired organic meaning; in short, it received a kind of psychological rehabilitation!

Bar 9

In this bar the answer enters in *A* minor in the middle voice; its reply to the subject entails unusual technical difficulties. On the one hand, the subject, opening on the dominant, demands an answer that opens on the tonic (the so-called *fuga tonale*, or "tonal" answer), i.e., a^1 answered by d^1. On the other hand, the distinctive shape of the subject demands a "real" answer if it is to remain intact; i.e., a^1 in the subject, the dominant of *D* minor, should be answered by its analogue, e^1, the dominant of *A* minor. Faced with this dilemma, Bach decided to combine the two answers, *a–d* and *a–e*, i.e., to answer a^1, the dominant of *D* minor, with d^1, the tonic of that key, but at the same time to leave room next to d^1 for e^1, the dominant of the new key (*A* minor).

The result is the unusual opening of the answer, in which both d^1 and e^1 are compressed into the space of one quarter note through the use of the rhythm .

Considering the fact that the sixth and eighth entrances (bars 76 and 107) begin in the same way (!),*[68] we must conclude that this opening configuration represents deliberate intent on Bach's part, an intent expressed so explicitly that a "correction," such as that undertaken by Bülow, is completely insupportable (see example 34).

Example 34

Indeed, this is a textbook example of editorial sacrilege! What could have led Bülow to correct Bach here, at a place of such importance, representing such an inspired solution? I am almost embarrassed to reveal that it was nothing but fear of—the seventh d^1-c^2! He took fright at this seventh which—*horribile dictu*—enters stark and unprepared; this alone struck terror into all his limbs! It is enough to make us laugh. I readily admit that I hold nothing against Bülow for giving no thought to Bach's reasoning (as outlined above)—nor do I take him to task for his ignorance of Bach's basic harmonic plan. Example 35 (in which I use the ghastly jargon of antiquated textbooks that still enjoy world-wide currency)[69] presents the underlying harmonies of bars 9-11, which make it clear that the seventh, c^2 (bar 9), is necessary to both harmonies for the purpose of creating a connection between them.

Example 35

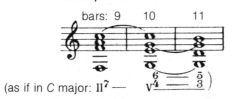

(as if in C major: II^7 — V$^6_4$ — $^5_3$)

As I said, I hold none of this against him, for such reasoning*[70] may well be too subtle for him. But what should one think when he does not even consult the evidence, the wholly external evidence so clearly provided by the composer himself at the sixth and eighth entrances? How can one forgive him for his failure to recall that the $F\sharp$-minor Fugue in Book I of the *Well-Tempered Clavier* introduces a similar seventh ($f\sharp$-e^1) at the entrance of the answer in the fourth bar? Can one credit Bülow with any general comprehension of the fugue when, as we see here, he was not even capable of separating and differentiating its two opposite poles, the subject and the answer?

Bar 10

Here we find a suspended fourth whose resolution does not take place until the next measure (bar 11), where it is transferred into the voice below (see example 36).

Example 36

Bar 16

The first episode (bars 16-18) is three measures long; it is based on the principal motive of the first countersubject (see bars 8 and 10).

Bar 17

The resolution of the suspended fourth, $\frac{c^2}{g^1}$, is again delayed until the next bar.[71]

Bar 19

At the third entrance (bars 19-26) the lower voice states the subject in D minor. The middle voice shows strict and complete adherence to the first countersubject, while the upper voice presents the second countersubject.

Bar 20

At the turn of bars 19-20 one should observe a feature of the voice leading—the effect produced when the upper voice moves down a fifth while the lower voice moves up a second (see example 37).

Example 37

bars: 19   20

This may be considered an example of a *quinta battuta*.[72]

Bar 26

The second episode (bars 26-41) effects the modulation to F major, states the cadence, and also provides the transition to the second section of the Fugue. Because of the considerable length of this episode, the fourth entrance occurs at some distance from the third entrance; this prevents the fourth entrance from sounding like a redundant entrance in the exposition. In other words, because of its length, the episode provides a particularly definitive separation between the second section and the first.

We encounter material derived from the first countersubject, first in the upper voice (bar 26), next in the lower voice (bars 27-30), and then in the upper voice again (bars 31-33).

Bar 27

In bars 27-29, observe the judicious use of eighth rests in the upper voice. These ventilating breathing spaces intensify the contrast created by the lengthy, sustained bb^2 of bar 30. Unfortunately, this and similar kinds of rests fell out of use long ago. Only a few of the truly great composers understood the benefits conferred by such rests. About a hundred years ago, musicians lost sight of the charm and benefit lent by such breathing rests, even to a purely instrumental line, as they became completely indifferent to the ill effects—the congealed and viscous line—that resulted from the absence of these rests. But are there any teachers that mention them? Are there any textbooks that discuss them?

Bar 31

The powerful motion by fifths of the preceding bars[73] (one need only observe the bass tones that open each bar: *e-A-d-G-c!*) may of course be further divided into motion by thirds: *e-(c)-A-(f)-d-(Bb)-G-(e)-c*. This is followed by a motion toward the subdominant of *F* major. The chromatic tone *Eb* heard at the I (see bar 31) tonicizes the IV;[*74] this *Eb* contributes to the greater effectiveness of the diatonic *E♮* at the V in bar 34.

Bar 36

The second episode continues and leads directly into the second section of the Fugue. It includes new, independent material. The first and third quarters in bars 36-40 determine the harmonic motion: an ascending step of a second is followed by a powerful descending fifth at the turn of each bar (see example 38).

Example 38

$$\frac{F\text{-}G}{}\Big/\frac{C\text{-}D}{}\Big/\frac{G\text{-}A}{}\Big/\frac{D\text{-}E}{}\Big/\frac{A\text{-}B}{E}$$

Bar 41

We have arrived at the second section of the Fugue and at the fourth entrance (bars 42-49). The middle voice states the subject in *A* minor. This entrance, however, contains a variation of the original statement of the fugal theme. Here, for the first time, the quarter notes of bars 5-6 appear in "diminution" as eighth notes (see the corresponding bars 46-47).[75]

The upper voice adheres to the first countersubject only where possible (see bars 43-45). In bar 46, one even finds that the lower counterpoint has abruptly taken over the *g*♯, which would properly have belonged in the upper voice, as its continuation.

But most notable is the lower counterpoint in bars 41 and 42. Its style seems out of character—fundamentally at variance with our concept of the fugue as the domain of "flowing melody"—and would be more appropriate in a homophonic setting. Yet how can we account for its appearance here? Perhaps it would be best to think of these two measures as the tail end of the bass motion of the preceding measures, a bass motion that may be considered more free, since it partakes of the relatively greater freedom of an episode. What a confluence of artistic logic and freedom; it is as if the bass tones of the episode have spilled over into the opening bars of the new entrance! The result is a stylistic equalization of episode and entrance, executed with Bach's unexcelled artistry.[76] Such consistency, such style!

Bar 46

If a trill is played in the left hand, then a suffix should be added.

Bar 49

The third episode (bars 49-59), like bars 36-41 of the second episode, includes new material.

Bar 57

A clue to the mystery behind this typically Bachian construction is provided by the bass motion on each eighth, for within the broad triadic entity extending from bar 57 to bar 59 (see example 39), this detailed motion expresses the chordal fragments (*Teilharmonien*) shown in example 40.

Example 39

bars: 57   58   59

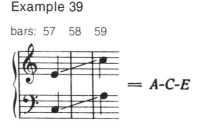

= A-C-E

49

Example 40

bar 57

1st—2nd eighths: *A—F♯*

3rd—4th eighths: .   . *B—G♯*

5th—6th eighths: .   .   . *C—A*   etc.

The scheme given in example 40 may be derived as follows. Let us first consider only the first and second eighths. Example 41 summates the triad that is composed out, *A-C-E*; the *g♯¹* (right hand) functions as a passing tone within the fourth e^1-a^1.[*77]

Example 41

The a^1, however, is not supported by a member of the *A-C-E* chord; instead, a foreign tone, *f♯*, suddenly appears in the bass. Or, to use terminology borrowed from the theory of counterpoint, the bass "moves on" (*fortschreitet*) before the first triad has been completed.[78] This new bass tone ushers in a second triad, *F♯-A-C* (see example 42).

Example 42

The third sixteenth note in the soprano, a^1, belongs to and completes the triad expressed at the first eighth c-e^1-(a^1); indeed, it serves to establish the existence of this triad. However, it is obvious that a^1 also belongs to the triad expressed at the second eighth, $f♯$-(a^1)-c^1. The same holds true at the second and third quarters; the third sixteenth note in the soprano belongs to the chords expressed at both the first and second eighths of each group.

Bar 59

One must admire the marvelous rhythmic technique (see example 43).

Example 43

bar 59

The tones that carry the melodic line occur a sixteenth note later in each group (see the first, second, and third sixteenth notes of the first, second, and third quarters). Had they been placed elsewhere, these same tones would have sounded wrong—who can imitate such a master?!

Bar 60

At the fifth entrance (bars 60-65 or 60-67), the subject is stated in *D* minor in the middle voice.

This entrance contains a variation similar to that found in the fourth entrance at bars 46-47. Here, however, the change in the fugal theme is more extensive; its final bars are omitted altogether. As a substitute for this omission, the fifth and sixth bars are repeated in bars 66-67, albeit in another voice, the upper voice. This kind of internal repetition within the fugal theme (and we will encounter similar repetition at the eighth and ninth entrances, the latter showing a far more subtle development) is not indigenous to the fugal domain; it is comparable to the type of repetition regularly used to enhance the continuity of homophonic compositions. Thus it is tinged with the flavor of imitative orchestral writing (e.g., imitation of the violin by the oboe); in short, there is a suggestion of story-telling, as though spinning a narrative!

Bar 60 recalls bar 42; the upper counterpoint contains figures that obviously derive from the preceding episode, figures that are not entirely characteristic of the fugal genre. What flexibility the composer shows toward the fugue! How unprejudiced is his attitude! Brahms is the only other composer whose approach is in any way comparable. For example, in the Fugue of his Handel Variations, op. 24, one finds polyphonic voices written in a purely idiomatic keyboard style, from which essential lines of an entirely contrapuntal nature may, of course, be derived (see example 44).[79]

Example 44: Brahms, Variations and Fugue on a Theme by Handel, Fugue, bar 33

How regrettable that textbooks on the fugue make no reference to the feasibility of such writing and are totally uninformative about the circumstances in which it would be appropriate!

Bar 64

A suffix could be added to the trill in the left-hand part.

Bar 68

We have reached the fourth episode (bars 68–75). Bars 68–71 obviously prepare for a half cadence on the dominant of *D* minor.

Bar 71

The trill in the left-hand part also calls for a suffix.

Bar 72

For this much-disputed measure, the Peters, Bülow, and Reinecke editions give the reading shown in example 45.

Example 45

This reading evidently derives from the feeling of half cadence: I and IV of bar 71 will surely be followed by V of the same key in bar 72, thus the chord *A-C♯-E*, its diatonic third *c♮²* raised to *c♯²* in confirmation of the half cadence.[80] At this chord— albeit in the opinion of the editors who give this reading—a modulation to *G* minor takes place; the V triad in *D* minor assumes the role of II in *G* minor, unaffected by the chromatic tones *C♯* and *E♮* (see example 46).[81]

Example 46

$$
\begin{array}{l}
D \text{ minor: } V\sharp \\
\hline
\phantom{D \text{ minor: }}{}^{\natural 5} \\
G \text{ minor: } II^{\sharp 3} \quad (—V^{\sharp 3}—I \text{ etc.})
\end{array}
$$

My own reading (which is the same as that found in the Bach-Gesellschaft, Bischoff, and Röntgen editions) also recognizes the listener's anticipation of a half cadence. However, this expectation is not fulfilled; at the V, a simple minor third, *c♮²*, is instantly substituted for the major third, *c♯²*. The resultant chord, *A-C♮-E*, serves as a more immediate and direct transition to *G* minor.

The two readings differ concerning the point at which *C♯* (as the third of the V chord in *D* minor) yields to *C♮* (as a diatonic note in *G* minor). The reading I favor assumes that *C♯* is merely sensed by the performer on the first quarter of bar 72; it is not actually sounded. The chromatic change is thus completed two quarters earlier than in the other reading, whose $C\sharp$ permits the actual occurrence of a half cadence in D minor, and whose diatonic $C\natural$ (in G minor) is reached only at the third quarter of bar 72.

Both readings are good. And if it were only a question of the harmony, one would have to say that the performer could do as he wished.

However, the evidence that points conclusively to our reading does not arise from the harmonic aspect of this passage. On making a detailed examination of the contents of bars 72-75, one suddenly becomes aware of a foreshadowing of the next entrance of the answer (bar 76)—the same kind of writing that one often finds in symphonic movements or in sonatas (see example 47).

Example 47

bars: 72-73   74-75   76-77

Therefore, in light of the task assigned to bars 72-73, the beginning of bar 72 must read $c\natural^2$-d^2, and not $c\sharp^2$-d^2—one feels this instinctively. However, this reading also has a completely rational basis; the most decisive reason for its adoption is that Bach's superb stylistic instinct, so innate and pervasive, would not have permitted him to present this thematic figure in a random, rambling succession—first in a complex form, then in a simpler one, and finally, in a third, once again complex version. This disorderly chain of events would occur if bar 72 were to begin with $c\sharp^2$, for then bars 72-73 would offer a complex portrayal of the figure, burdened with a modulation (see above); by contrast, bars 74-75 would depict the simple figure (without a modulation), and finally, bars 76-77 would follow, their chromatic motion revealing a renewed and heightened complexity. Bach is much more likely to proceed from the simple to the complex (and this is what he judiciously chose to do here). The application of this principle demands the use of $c\natural^2$ in bar 72, for it permits the harmonic settings of the first and second figures (bars 72-73 and bars 74-75) to be equal in their simplicity: II-V-I in G minor and II-V-I in D minor. The succeeding measures may then confidently proceed to more complex events![*82]

Bar 73

The tie shown in example 48, omitted in many editions (Bischoff, Reinecke, and Röntgen) is not only an abstract possibility but is also a concrete contrapuntal necessity—it permits the rhythm of the middle voice to take prominence.[83]

Example 48

bar 73

Bar 76

At the sixth entrance (bars 76-83), the answer is stated in B minor in the lower voice.

Bars 5-7 of the fugal theme—appearing here as bars 80-82—are again fragmented through diminution. A close and careful comparison of this entrance with the preceding fourth and fifth entrances, which also exhibit diminution, will reveal a difference in the diminution of bars 80-81. The precise nature of the change may easily be observed if one transposes bars 46-47 and bars 64-65 to B minor and compares these transposed versions with bars 80-81. What pursuit of diversity!

The countersubjects are new; there is just a trace of the first countersubject near the end, in bar 81.

Bar 80

The trill requires a suffix. The middle voice rests!

Bar 83

In the fifth episode (bars 83-89), we find that bars 83-86 are shaped entirely out of material derived from the first countersubject, including even the figures in the bass of bars 85-86—the original motive is revealed when one leaves out the second sixteenth-note of each four-note group.

Bar 85

A reading of $g\sharp^2$ is obligatory for the first quarter note of this measure. This note should be understood as part of the chord E-$G\sharp$-$B\natural$; it descends chromatically to $g\natural^2$ only at the third quarter. The necessity for $g\sharp^2$ has its basis in the chromatic line shown in example 49, a chromatic line that no one but Bach could conceive and beautifully sustain, overcoming every obstacle![*84]

Example 49

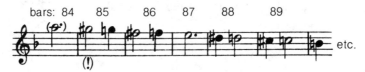

bars: 84   85   86   87   88   89

Accordingly, the $g\natural^2$ given in the Bach-Gesellschaft edition, as well as by Bischoff and Röntgen, is wrong.[85] The eighth rests in the upper voice of bars 84-86 may be compared to those in bars 27-29.[86]

Bar 88

The composer's marvelous consistency is evident in the first quarter of this measure: he writes $c\sharp^1$ in the lower voice even though it coincides with $c\natural^2$ in the middle voice!

But it could not be otherwise! Again, it is the harmonic motion that provides an explanation (that of bars 87-89; see example 50).[87]

Example 50

bars: 87 — 88 — 89
C-A — B$^{\sharp 3}$-E$^{\sharp 3}$ — A$^{\sharp 3-\natural 3}$ etc.

Example 51 provides a sketch of the three voices of bar 88, with the latent root added.

Example 51

bar 88

9 — 8
$\sharp$5 — $\sharp$6
$\sharp$3 - $\natural$3

We realize that c^2 in the second highest voice forms a suspension of a ninth over the true root of the chord that governs the first and second quarters, i.e., a ninth measured from $B\natural$. (In the piece itself, the composing-out process causes this root to be delayed until the second quarter!) The resolution to $b\natural^1$ does not take place until the third quarter; it is preceded by a detour through the inserted chord tone $f\sharp^1$, in total conformity with the rules of strict counterpoint. In the text of the composition the notes $f\sharp$-$b\natural$-$g\sharp$ constitute the lowest voice; in the sketch they appear in an inner voice (as if in the tenor). It is this voice, however, that is composed out and ornamented in the text of the piece; example 52 demonstrates how the composing-out process is applied to the first quarter.

Example 52

for: thus:
etc. etc.

Instead of being stated at the interval of a second (as e), the second sixteenth note is written as a seventh (e^1), which is quite the same thing.[*88] At the third sixteenth note $d\sharp^1$ must be used, in conformity with the first quarter's implicit major third, manifest as $d\sharp^2$ in the top voice. (Only in the second quarter will it drop down to a minor third, through mixture.) It is the task of the fourth and final sixteenth note to create a bridge between $d\sharp^1$ and $b\natural$, i.e., to provide a transition to the first sixteenth note of the next quarter. It is self-evident that $d\sharp^1$-$c\sharp^1$ is much more appropriate than the augmented second $d\sharp^1$-$c\natural^1$! This accounts for the so-called "cross-relation" between $c\natural^2$ and $c\sharp^1$ in this measure.*[89]

Bar 90

At the seventh entrance (bars 90-96) the subject is stated in E minor in the upper voice.

Yet another new countersubject appears in the middle voice (bars 90-93). Its bold figuration is most beautifully entwined with the subject's melodic line. Of course, the sixteenth notes of this new countersubject are stylistically related to the sixteenth notes of the preceding episode.*[90] One should not overlook the delightful hemiola that results from the motivic organization of the sixteenth-note groups in bars 92-93 (♩♩ ♩|♩ ♩♩). What artistry!

But how magnificent is the starting point of bar 94, with its sudden eruption of long-restrained passion; it is as if our ears were showered with the lava of thickened polyphony![91] One might question such a sudden profusion of voices in a three-voice fugue—is there not a contradiction here? No! For in the hands of a master the fugue has ever and always been different from fugal form as conceived in schools and text-books, past and present!

Of course, Bach would not have been the master that he was, and indeed this profusion of voices would be unconvincing—like a mere whim—had he not provided detailed advance preparation for the effect he wished to achieve. One should note the uninterrupted, agitated sixteenth notes in bars 87-93 and the threatening organ point that begins in bar 90! And finally, the most inspired stroke: Bach intentionally deletes the last eighth note in the fourth bar of the fugal theme, as if forcibly stifling the voice leading's drive toward a purely contrapuntal continuation! One must grasp the superhuman quality of Bach's musical instinct; if the final $b\natural^1$ were present, the voice would flow on quietly, sure of its destination; but without $b\natural^1$ the sound comes to an abrupt halt at the third quarter—a stoppage that is all the more compelling because of its unexpectedness, considering the previous behavior of the fugal theme. Bach's deliberate planning is most clearly demonstrated at the analogous place in the ninth entrance (bar 134), where the same effect should and must be achieved with even greater boldness! But this inspired stroke was lost on Bischoff and Bülow; they all simply reinstate the $b\natural^1$ . . .[92]

Aside from this change in the fourth bar of the fugal theme, an additional change in its seventh bar—appearing here as bar 96—must be noted.[93]

Also of importance is the knowledge that without the added fillers,[94] bars 94-95 would proceed as in example 53, which shows the essential three-voice setting.

Example 53

bars: 94   95

etc.

Bar 97

The sixth episode (bars 97-106) should be compared with the fourth episode.[95]

Bar 107

At the eighth entrance (bars 107-112 or 107-114) the answer appears in the middle voice, in *D* minor. The fugal theme is stated only as far as its sixth measure (bar 112 here); the fifth and sixth measures are repeated, as in the fifth entrance.

Several further alterations of the fugal theme should be noted. In the second measure, the leap of a sixth is composed out. In the third measure a dotted rhythm is used, similar to that of the first measure; the same dotted rhythm replaces the two eighth notes in the third quarter of the fourth measure.

Bar 111

A suffix could be added to the trill.

Bar 115

The seventh episode (bars 115-130) begins here. Familiar material is supplemented by much that is new (see bars 118-125). The two-voice texture in bars 120-121 should be noted.

Bar 126

Observe the chromatic descent in the middle voice (see example 54).[*96]

Example 54

Bar 131

At the ninth entrance (bars 131-136 or 131-138) the subject appears in the middle voice, in *G* minor!

The configuration of the fugal theme is reminiscent of the seventh entrance (bar 90 ff.). Here too, in the theme's fourth bar (bar 134), the second eighth of the third quarter is omitted (cf. bar 93) and, as before, there is an eruption into thickened polyphony.[97] But these similarities only serve to point up the differences between the two versions. In the seventh entrance, the first six measures of the fugal theme remained in one voice, the upper voice (bars 90-95); in the ninth entrance, on the other hand, the middle voice states only four measures of the theme (bars 131-134), and the fifth and sixth measures (bars 135-136) are then abruptly transferred to another voice, the upper voice! (The principle that guides this bold procedure is obviously the exchange of voices.) It is easy to see that Bach had even more cause here, in the ninth entrance, to omit the previously mentioned second eighth note of the third quarter in bar 4 of the fugal theme (bar 134); for this eighth-note d^1 would have sounded harsh and out of place as a passing tone that is continued in another, higher, voice. Thus we are given another opportunity to admire Bach's sensitive adherence to logical order—he proceeds from the simple to the complex, in this case from the relatively simpler setting of the seventh entrance to the more complex ninth entrance!

Aside from the exchange of voices mentioned above, one must of course point out that the fugal theme is stated only as far as its sixth measure (bar 136). The remaining bars are replaced by a repetition of the fifth and sixth measures (bars 135-136), as was the case in the fifth and eighth entrances. However, Bach has endowed even the repetition with a sudden new meaning—it is bolder and more complex than before. In the fifth and eighth entrances, the function of the repeated bars was merely to compensate for the curtailment of the fugal theme. Here they serve the surprising additional function—what inspired technique!—of effecting a modulation to D minor in bar 137, and then, within the frame of a single measure (bar 139), to A minor! This new treatment may be traced to the loosened cohesion of the theme's first six bars, which are now performed by two voices in succession. The separated fifth and sixth bars are thus much more independent and lend themselves quite naturally to bolder development. It is evident that the repeated measures also serve as the eighth episode!

Bar 137

Concerning the eighth episode (bars 137-139), see the end of my discussion under the heading of bar 131, above.

Bar 140

At the tenth entrance (bars 140-145), the subject appears in the lower voice, in D minor. Otherwise, the same situation obtains as in the sixth entrance.

Here the bass entrance may be doubled in octaves *ad libitum*!

Bar 147

The ninth episode begins here (cf. bar 118 ff.).

Bar 154

At the eleventh and last entrance (bars 154-159), the subject is stated in the upper voice, in D minor. This entrance, deliberately placed in the highest register, forms a most effective contrast with the penultimate (tenth) entrance placed in the lowest register! This statement of the subject extends through the sixth measure of the fugal theme (bar 159). To intensify the strong drive toward the close, majestic added voices appear in bars 158 and 159 (as they did in bars 94 and 135 ff.). Moreover, in the fourth measure of the fugal theme (bar 157 here)—in spite of the approaching thickened polyphony—the second eighth note of the third quarter is reinstated; it assumes its original rightful place. There you have it: the liberties that were completely justified in the middle section and at the beginning of the closing section here yield to the higher necessity of restating the subject in its original, intact form at the end of the Fugue!

Bar 160

Lastly, the free ending in bar 160[*98] requires the freest performance of the run and the trill! The run should be played in a free declamatory manner, especially at the beginning. (This will be aided by adherence to the suggested fingering!) The trill should end near the last sixteenth note, or better yet, just on it (see the execution I suggest in the score);[*99] on no account should its ending coincide with the chord. To be sure, the final sixteenth note, d^1, is then abridged to a thirty-second note, perhaps even to a sixty-fourth note! Example 55 presents another closing trill, occurring at the end of Bach's Organ Fugue in C major.[100] In spite of the difference between the even and dotted rhythm, the execution shown here (in the notation given by Liszt in his transcription)[*101] will shed some light on the execution suggested for the closing trill of our Fugue.

Example 55: Bach, Organ Fugue in C Major (Liszt)

The table of entrances given at the start of these annotations (see table I) served as a guide to the course of the Fugue. However, I feel it would be useful to add a concise schematic summary at this point, in order to provide a clearer visual picture of the fugal plan (see table II).[*102]

TABLE II

Voices	bars 1-8	bars 9-16	bars 19-26	bars 42-49	bars 60-65	bars 76-83	bars 90-95	bars 107-112	bars 131-136	bars 140-145	bars 154-159
upper voice	(1) subject D minor						(7) subject E minor				(11) subject D minor
middle voice		(2) answer A minor		(4) subject A minor	(5) subject D minor			(8) answer D minor	(9) subject G minor		
lower voice			(3) subject D minor			(6) answer B minor				(10) subject D minor	

Section I   Section II   Section III

The diagram (table II) shows that the fugal theme enters three times in the upper voice, five times in the middle voice, and another three times in the lower voice. These entrances may be tabulated as follows:

upper voice   subject $\begin{cases} D \text{ minor} \\ E \text{ minor (not } A \text{ minor!)} \\ D \text{ minor} \end{cases}$

middle voice   subject $\begin{cases} A \text{ minor} \\ D \text{ minor} \\ G \text{ minor} \end{cases}$

         answer $\begin{cases} A \text{ minor} \\ D \text{ minor} \end{cases}$

lower voice   subject $\begin{cases} D \text{ minor} \\ D \text{ minor} \end{cases}$

         answer B minor (not A minor!)

The following additional summary lists the intervals created at each entrance:[103]

Entrance No.

2 (answer) 7

3 . . . . $\frac{8}{6}$

4 . . . . $\frac{8}{5}{3}$

5 . . . . $\frac{8}{3}$

6 . . . . $\frac{6}{3}$

7 . . . . $\frac{6}{5}$

8 . . . . $\frac{8}{3}$

9 . . . . $\frac{6}{5}$ (or $\frac{7}{3}$)

10 . . . . $\frac{8}{3}$

11 . . . . $\frac{5}{4}$

Even this aspect exhibits great variety and diversity.

*   *   *

The following conclusions may be drawn from my discussion of the Fugue:

1. Since the primary function of the first part of the Fugue is the solid establishment of the fugal theme, both as subject and answer, Bach has the good judgment to avoid varying it here. Any alteration would certainly confuse the listener about the theme's original shape and dimensions. However, in the remainder of the Fugue, Bach casts off the now superfluous ballast of these once meaningful and sensitive self-imposed constraints and allows changes to be made (in either subject or answer). The contrast and variety provided by these changes actually clarify the essence of the fugal theme, as when Bach embellishes it (with diminutions or the like), abridges it, or expands it by means of repetition.

2. The episodes retain their inherent freedom, yet Bach takes every opportunity to bring about stylistic balance between episode and entrance, in spite of the divergence of these fugal elements. In other words, he carefully avoids an awkward and abrupt juxtaposition of the conflicting characters of entrance and episode.

3. In general, Bach adheres to his chosen number of voices. But he is not strictly bound by his choice—artistic considerations often lead him to use fewer voices (e.g., in order to lighten the texture, obtain greater fluidity, etc.) or to use a greater number (e.g., in order to intensify the pathos, etc.).

4. Bach shows similar adherence to the first countersubject, but applies the principle of variety where appropriate. This flexibility permits the exchange of voices and the like.

These few items will suffice. To summarize briefly:

Bach subjects the various elements of the Fugue only to those constraints that must obtain in every situation and that are fundamental to the fugal form. Beyond this he exercises the fullest freedom.

Now that we have defined the characteristics of a Bach fugue, we know what a fugue really is—what it should be and what it should not be! Schumann's remark comes to mind: "The shallowest mind tries to hide behind a fugue. Fugues are the province of none but the greatest masters!"[104] The actual facts bear out the truth of this statement, perhaps to an even greater degree than Schumann himself suspected. In the last analysis, after Bach only the greatest among great composers achieved absolute mastery of the fugue—only Haydn, Mozart, Beethoven, Mendelssohn, and Brahms.[105] If Schubert and Schumann failed to achieve such mastery—without detriment to their greater accomplishments in other areas—then what should one say of the many, far too many others whose musical intelligence, imagination, and creative ability is meager at best?!

This form has been plagued by the mechanical writing of amateurs; soulless activity will never produce a genuine fugue. One cannot simply slip into Bach's garment and busily write fugues or chorale preludes, for if the setting is clumsy and the material is given amateurish treatment, then truly nothing is left of the fugue but its title.

Incompetent teachers undoubtedly share the blame with altogether deficient textbooks. Such teachers, themselves possessing minimal insight and minimal artistic perception, do the younger generation a grave injustice by imparting and implanting only this bare minimum. Although this situation is often genuinely unavoidable, teachers frequently create it intentionally, offering the explanation that students of average talent should be given only average instruction. I maintain that anyone who makes such a statement is immediately suspect; obviously his artistic gifts are insufficient—he *must* resort to this excuse! Anyone who himself is more than minimally competent will surely maintain that it is more reasonable—and far more pedagogically sound—to teach the younger generation as much of the truth as possible and to teach it in the best possible way, leaving it up to them to grasp as much as their intellectual capacity permits. Those who give should always be generous—those who receive will always discover their own limitations!

3. NON-LEGATO

In performing this work, as in most early works, one should generally use a "non-legato" touch.[*106] If one imagines how this composition would sound when played on the violin, one quickly realizes that its contents are basically incompatible with true violinistic legato, although at times legato phrasing does seem to be called for.

Let me say just this much about non-legato here: While tones may be given highly varied shading—and how this is achieved must remain the performer's private secret—ideally, each tone should nonetheless be given its own individual weight and pressure; only by means of such articulation may true non-legato be differentiated from staccato on the one hand and from genuine legato (or legatissimo) on the other. To gain a better understanding of this kind of touch, one may draw a parallel with the so-called *détaché* of violin technique: *grand détaché* calls for each tone to be played by the whole bow, while in *moyen détaché* only about a third of the bow is used. Or one might think of organ sound, which excludes true legato in the strictest sense. Thus it is clear that non-legato touch is achieved primarily by giving each individual tone a separate and distinct articulation. Of course, the duration assigned to each tone by the composer remains unchanged; the note values should never be curtailed!

The use of this kind of touch automatically results in a more moderate tempo. Non-legato is incompatible with a rapid tempo, especially with a very rapid tempo; the same is true of genuine legato, since when using either touch one can easily, often unwittingly, slip into a kind of staccato, particularly in florid passages and runs.

One should not forget that the performance of early works, besides requiring the distinct articulation of individual tones, often calls for another kind of technique, that of holding down the keys by leaving the fingers on them. This technique is applicable not only to the performance of arpeggios and other similarly broken figures (see the Fantasy, bar 12, left hand; bar 75, right hand; and the Fugue, bar 60),[107] but also to figures and melismas comprising only stepwise motion (e.g., in the Fugue, c^2 in the second quarter of bar 17, right hand, should be played as if it were a dotted eighth note; d^2 in the second quarter of bar 69, right hand, should be given the same duration).[*108] When tones are sustained in this way, a uniquely warm effect is produced. This very attractive kind of legato, unlike simple legato, is not limited to the connection of two consecutive tones; it may also create a close link between tones that do not follow each other immediately, but are separated by intervening tones. Of course, this subtle technique—known to so few virtuoso performers—cannot be indicated by any notational symbol. The use of the legato slur, with its strong motivic implications, would be misleading, since this is a purely acoustic technique.

In conclusion, it is self-evident that legatissimo is highly appropriate in recitative passages. One should imagine a violinist drawing his bow, a singer taking long breaths, and likewise make the keyboard sing the recitative sections!

4. DYNAMICS

A discussion of dynamics must be preceded by a consideration of the following question:

If a work by Bach—and here the reader may include works by other composers of this early period—contains very few dynamic indications (e.g., the Fantasy)[109] or none at all (e.g., the Fugue) should one assume that the dynamic shading Bach desired was as sparse as his explicit indications; i.e., that there were to be no dynamic shading at all in the Fugue? Or did Bach have different intentions?

Musicians of our time give various responses:

One group—consisting primarily of conductors and virtuoso pianists—favors the belief that if no indications are present, the entire work should simply be performed in a uniform *forte*, without any subtle deviations. If there are a few original indications, these should be strictly observed, again avoiding any intermediate gradations; *forte* is interpreted as a uniform *forte*, *piano* as a uniform *piano*, each holding sway regardless of context, until one indication is supplanted by another. These musicians claim faithfulness to the original as their guiding principle.

Another group of musicians—consisting mainly of editors—takes a different view. While acknowledging that the original texts of the early masters are devoid of dynamic shading in the abstract and historical sense, they believe that one must nevertheless bow to an overwhelming need for variegated shading, a necessity that arose in the post-Bach era and is particularly strong today. Thus—mind you, only to fulfill the aforementioned need!—they blithely add the gaudiest dynamic indications to the original text.

Which group is right? Unfortunately, neither; this question requires a completely different answer.

While the original text may include some or lack all dynamic indications, any indications must unquestionably be supplemented by innumerable dynamic nuances. In earlier times, directives for the introduction of such nuances were almost always given orally, though they were sometimes included in theoretical treatises.[*110] Custom required that this oral or written instruction be reflected in performance, especially where the composer gave no indications for dynamics. Thus one must concede that the original score appears "unmarked" only to those who are unfamiliar with these teachings whereas those who, like musicians of earlier times, still follow these teachings today recognize the score's rich potential for dynamic shading. Indeed they will find that it contains a veritable surplus of nuances for which no indications are given![111] This situation is entirely different from that reflected in the views of the two groups of musicians described above!

A clearer understanding of this situation may be gained by making an analogy with current pedal technique. I ask the following question: If someone were to criticize us for using the pedal in performances of Beethoven sonatas, could this critic find any justification in the fact that Beethoven himself did not notate any (or at best only a few) pedal signs? There is no doubt that we would repudiate this criticism; we would reply that instruction in the use of the pedal is usually transmitted orally (from teacher to student) and that Beethoven, as aware of this pedagogical practice as we are, could leave decisions regarding pedalling to the performer, who would then be answerable for them. In actual fact a theory of pedalling does exist; its basic (and execrable) minimum requirement is that each chord change be accompanied by a change of pedal. But defying any description is that delicate, supremely delicate artistic pedal technique which goes far beyond this minimal rule, and which is practiced only by the most imaginative performer. While such pedalling is not expressly indicated by the composer, it would undoubtedly meet with his approval. Thus we would be completely justified in repudiating the above criticism and in regarding it as the absurd consequence of hypocritical piety.

However, what strikes me as equally absurd are the positions taken by the afore-mentioned first group of musicians—when they proudly boast of their fidelity to the original, when they argue that the composer would have marked his score differently if he had really wanted it to be different, or when they insist (probably in order to sound impressive) that the early masters wished to highlight the "construction" of their music by rejecting all nuances as petty distractions. How could the proponents of such ideas overlook the important fact that this earlier period was characterized by pietistic emotionalism? How can they fail to ask themselves why our ancestors built such large organs, capable of producing such richly colorful sounds, or why they sought to provide their stringed keyboard instruments with different registers and devices for producing *crescendo*? And why should one ascribe to such a master as Bach the kind of music that rolls evenly along with unvarying monotony—when every note in his Passions and cantatas demonstrates his ability to give the most complex moods and meanings their utmost expression in music? I say it is time to banish such orthodoxy! From a purely practical point of view, it invites the charge that this sham artistic fidelity to the original conceals a deficiency, since it offers the easiest and least arduous approach to the text. A uniform, monotonous, mechanical performance, *f = forte, p = piano*—what could be easier, especially if one convinces oneself (and perhaps others also) that the master has thus been rendered his due!

As to the other group of musicians, namely the editors, one need only repudiate their basic premise and admonish them for thinking that they do Bach a service by improving his music and making it more beautiful than he or his contemporaries could have imagined. No indeed! *They* are beholden to Bach; in principle they owe him at least as much homage as that given him by his contemporaries—and I have not even touched on the question of whether today's performances are as good as those of former times.

My own position in regard to the question of dynamics is best demonstrated by the dynamic markings given in my edition.[112]

We now come to a more specific question: the meaning of *forte*.

Since *forte* is required so frequently in performing the Fantasy, one must guard against mistaken notions of the term's meaning. It is widely and erroneously believed that *forte* is a purely acoustical phenomenon, a physical quantity of sound whose intensity remains homogeneous and unchanged until supplanted by *piano*. When will it finally be understood that the indication *f* may comprise the same dynamic shadings as *p*?! One should not be afraid of giving the sign *f* the same treatment as *p* (with which performers have always been more comfortable) and yield to each expressive exigency, even to the point of reaching *piano* as the outer limit of *forte*. One need not be afraid that the overall impression of *forte* would be obscured by such shading—as long as it is used at the right time and in the appropriate situation. The use of shading is advisable if for physiological reasons alone; the ear welcomes contrast even within higher levels of intensity, and soon becomes stultified by a long stretch of *forte*! Thus such shadings are not merely permissible; they are an absolute necessity! One should therefore strive for intellectual understanding of *forte* and finally come to regard it as a psychological phenomenon rather than a mere physical quantity! It would be high time!

This is what the great masters had in mind when they used the symbols *f*, *sf*, or even ———— at single notes or groups of notes within a passage governed by a general indication of *f* or *ff*.[*113] But when we hear our conductors, performers of chamber music, etc., continue an initial *f* or *ff* at a uniform level without any shadings, we can only be appalled by the paucity of their artistic instincts. They are completely insensitive to the stultifying effect of an extended stretch of unrelieved *forte*; indeed, they shamelessly believe that the composer himself had precisely this effect in mind. They assume—and this is amply demonstrated by their performances—that the renewed appearances of the sign *f* are intended to serve as a simple reminder of the continuing existence of *forte*. It would never occur to them that the broad dynamic integrity could still be maintained if these symbols represented accents that are actually more prominent, accents that must be brought to the attention of the listener, reaching his ear with convincing psychological force. Surely this effect can be achieved in no other way than by endeavoring to drain off, as it were, the *f* that surrounds the *f* accents, and to give those surrounding *f* passages a more subdued rendition. The general and specific expressivity is heightened by the true psychological effectiveness of such dynamic relief; moreover, the composer's intent is realized!

I should, indeed I must, take this opportunity to mention the following passage from a letter by Brahms (as imparted by Franz Fridberg in the *Vossische Zeitung* of April 3, 1907), discussing the opening bars of Brahms's String Quintet in *G* major: "You may tell him [the cellist] he has every right to demand that, starting in the third and fourth measures, at least the two violins should merely feign their *f*! Thus they can favor him with a really nice *mf*; he can repay them later in the movement with a most beautiful *p*."[114] Fridberg goes on to relate a conversation in which Brahms took part: "During a discussion of the various gradations of *forte* and *piano*, I heard Brahms assert that *piano* could exist even within *forte*. When someone ventured to find this contradictory, Brahms cut him off mid-word with 'nonsense,' opened a newspaper that was on the table, and took no further part in the conversation." Indeed, the composer's indifference was entirely justified. How misguided are the ignorant in their tiresome, unwavering campaign against contradiction! Again, we are faced with those ugly and paradoxical dealings of lesser intellects, who seem to take pleasure in imposing their envy and ideas about contradiction only upon greater minds. And they make their accusations at the very moment they are being granted a singular and subtle insight! This could indeed be considered a verbal counterpart of the efforts of those editors who do not even attempt to emend the works of lesser talents, but are always ready to correct those of the masters. If our ignorant listener had been offered the same advice by a *Kapellmeister* or a virtuoso performer rather than by Brahms, then, you may be sure, he would have accepted it gratefully and unhesitatingly! He happily and trustingly takes even the worst advice offered by conductors and virtuosos—who in the Nietzchean sense are truly the "actors" in our artistic world! [115] When will the public finally perceive that only the great masters, those who have contributed to the history of composition—Handel, J. S. Bach, C.P.E Bach, Mozart, Beethoven, Schumann, Mendelssohn, Chopin, and Brahms—are also the sole contributors to the history of interpretive technique? By contrast, the so-called virtuosos, the "famous" and the "very famous," have made no serious contribution, not even in the area of pure interpretation. Virtuoso performers receive finished works from the masters; yet they vainly and presumptuously pass them off as their own technical triumphs. This is inevitable in a profession directed solely toward such triumphs, a profession which requires the continual exercising of one's hands in the tonal regions of others. Surely these virtuosos—in spite of their technical proficiency (Hieronymus says: "*non voce, sed corde cantandum est.*"!) [116]— fall short in every important obligation to the works they perform. For when left to themselves, they often do not even know what *forte* means! [*117]

It would be impossible to notate all the gradations of *forte*; the performer must therefore supply them himself. Occasionally, and only where it seemed absolutely necessary, I have added the signs ⸺⸺ and ⸺⸺ , to suggest a relative increase or decrease of *f*.

Incidentally, it is not wrong to interpret the sign *p*—my edition includes those thought to be authentic—as a kind of shading within *forte*, rather than as a truly distinct contrast to passages marked *f*. [*118]

5. FINGERING

The fingering indicated in my edition has a psychological basis. By this I mean that the fingering I have chosen should, through the grouping it suggests, divulge the organic connection or, conversely, the separation of the notes. A careful study of my choice of fingering will surely convince the performer that fingering—giving the word its most comprehensive definition—can actually provide a key to the inner meaning of a work.[119] A few examples will suffice to explain this statement.[120]

1. In order to achieve motivic separation, the fourth finger of the left hand is indicated for two successive notes—see bar 23 of the Fantasy, the last thirty-second note of the second quarter and the first thirty-second note of the third quarter: A-$B\natural$. A similar function is served by the successive use of the third finger for the notes $c\sharp^2$-$g\sharp^1$ in the last quarter of bar 61.

2. In order to intensify the expressivity, the thumb is indicated more frequently than in normal usage, as in the Fantasy, bar 12, left hand; bar 19 (at the turn of bars 19-20); bar 26, right hand; and bar 50.

3. When a group of repeated notes is given a different fingering at the repetition, the change in fingering aims to alter the tone color. Examples may be found in the Fantasy, bar 6, third and fourth quarters, left hand: 3-4-2-3|1; bar 18, left hand; bar 23, right hand; bar 24, right hand; and also in the Fugue, bar 48, left hand; bar 81, right hand.[121]

4. To achieve a poetic effect, the pedantic rules governing the use of the thumb are deliberately disregarded. In the Fantasy, bar 56 provides an example (in going from the third to the fourth quarter of the measure). In the third quarter of bar 57, a^1 definitely requires the fourth finger rather than the thumb; the second finger must then glide over the fourth in order to play the succeeding $b\natural^1$. (Similarly, the fourth finger follows the fifth in moving from the last note of bar 60 to the first note of bar 61!) In the Fugue, examples may be found at bar 114 (!), left hand; bar 115 (!), right hand; and bar 120. In general, it would be very instructive to compare the fingering found in my edition with that given by others. In the Fantasy, examples that merit such comparison may be found in bars 1, 3, 17, 63-67, etc.; in the Fugue, in bars 27-30, 39 (!), 90-91, 93 (!!), 108 (!), 131, etc., etc.[122]

The silent change of finger on the same key, as is required in bars 76 and 77 of the Fantasy, must be given very special consideration here. In spite of assurances to the contrary offered by J. S. Bach and C.P.E. Bach, in spite of the achievements of Mozart, Beethoven, Chopin, or Brahms as performers, so highly acclaimed by their contemporaries, in spite of all this, the world cannot rid itself of its prejudice: it is still universally believed that keyboard instruments cannot be made to sing! Surely it is obvious that pianists who have achieved true mastery of the keyboard have always recognized its potential as a singing instrument. Indeed, this potential has been denied only by pianists whose technical inspiration and energy are insufficient, and because of this insufficiency the piano has failed to assume its rightful place beside the violin and the human voice. Hearing a virtuoso play, one is horrified to find that a human soul can bear such a close resemblance to the mechanical workings of the piano; the sounds are so stiff, the colors so gray. This type of performer clings to the delusion that a tone produced by the piano is irrevocably defined by the initial attack; thereafter it reverberates only for a brief moment, regrettably immutable and sterile! Poor soul, he is completely unaware of the fact that a pianist (in spite of the nature of piano sound, which is of course different from vocal or violin sound) possesses an ability that is generally believed to be the prerogative of a singer or a violinist—the ability to spin out a tone![123] While it is true that the manner in which this is done by a singer (through his breath) or a violinist (through his bow) is different, it is nonetheless true that a pianist also has the means to produce this effect. Leaving aside the countless artifices afforded by undulations of the lower arm, I make this plea: Let a pianist try just once to replace one finger with another while holding down the same key, i.e., while still sounding the same tone. (What a pity that pianists as yet have no inkling of this technique!) And this should be done not for the sake of effecting a smoother connection to the subsequent fingering (that kind of finger change has a completely different significance), nor for purposes of legatissimo performance.[*124] Rather, the pianist should take delight in the action for its own sake, since it allows him to focus on the tone beyond its initial attack. In this spirit, if he permits one finger to replace the other by silently sliding it onto the same key, he will experience the sensation—naturally this is a subjective phenomenon that is at first felt by him alone—that he is actually spinning out his tone in the same way that a singer or violinist spins out his. And now a miracle is performed: this illusory subjective phenomenon is transformed into an objective occurrence, clearly audible to the listener! That is to say, the listener senses a unique warmth, a singing tone, even though the pianist is expressing his intimate relation to the tone first of all within the private sphere of his own feelings! The variety of ways in which this is achieved—by such heterogeneous means as breath, bow, and change of finger—may simply be ascribed to the differences between the instruments. But one should not rush the changing of fingers; rather, the tone should be spun out in tranquility and joy!

In conclusion, I should add that in questions of fingering Praetorius's old truth still holds: it makes no difference *how* one does it; even the nose may assist, as long as the proper meaning is conveyed![*125] There is more truth in this assertion than in the widespread teachings of the school of fingering whose adherents, because of ignorance or lack of understanding, prescribe a succession of fingers wholly determined by external criteria. Though detrimental to the music, this kind of fingering gives the external visual impression that it satisfies the demands made by the printed page. The above-mentioned school of fingering embraces only one rule—yet another "minimum": Unencumbered by any concern for the psychological basis of such motions as turning the thumb under the fingers or crossing the fingers over the thumb, the adherents of this school are guided only by the distance that needs to be covered, by the number of notes that will follow in the given hand position, and the like. They are completely unaware that these proceedings can only serve to mechanize and deaden the senses of the performer. They show no concern for the injury done to the work by this mechanical performance. Indeed, due to their meager understanding of the composer's wishes (i.e., their ignorance of the true content of the composition), they are oblivious to the fact that any damage has been done at all.

I will go so far as to maintain that respect for the "modern" style of Liszt or Rubinstein—so highly admired as the apparent apex of technique—would quickly evaporate if one could only comprehend and appreciate the original fingerings of such composers as J. S. Bach,[*126] C.P.E. Bach, Beethoven,[*127] Chopin,[*128] Schumann,[*129] and Brahms![*130] What a completely different world! Yet precisely these original fingerings are so readily sacrificed by editors in the presumption that they can replace them with better ones! And these supposed improvements of editors are then supplemented by the supposed improvements of virtuoso performers! The great pity of it is that these shallow virtuosos, who have never devised or employed comparable fingerings, have managed to convince the public (to the great detriment of our artistic endeavors) that they are better and greater pianists than the composers themselves, that they are pianists κατ' ἐξοχήν (pianists *par excellence*)! Within the steady decline in the general cultivation of music, this one specialty has sunk so low that those who now wish to learn to play the piano feel ashamed to play "only" as well as Beethoven, Mozart, Mendelssohn, Chopin, and Brahms; they wish to play much better, perhaps as well as Emil Sauer, or someone like him! Indeed, state and society—regardless of cost—take pride in educating our young people after the model of these shallow virtuosos! They imagine they are fostering culture, but they are in fact entrusting the younger generation to ignorant men who, compared to the masters, have very little awareness of the true nature and riches of the instrument.

Notes for the Introduction and the Commentary

The notes marked with an asterisk (*) either were originally part of Schenker's text or were added by Jonas in his revised edition. The translator's notes and additions are enclosed in square brackets.

[1. J. S. Bach, *Werke*, complete edition of the Bach-Gesellschaft, vol. 36, ed. by Ernst Naumann (Leipzig: Breitkopf & Härtel, 1890), hereafter referred to as the BG edition.

Schenker's own copy of this volume is part of the Oster Collection, housed in the Music Division of the New York Public Library, Special Collections. The volume lacks the pages containing the Chromatic Fantasy and Fugue (pp. 71-80); these pages, bearing many indications in Schenker's hand, are located in a separate folder—designated in Ernst Oster's typewritten catalogue of the collection as "Das Original der Chromatischen Fantasie u. Fuge zur Schenker-Ausgabe." Schenker evidently removed these pages from his copy of the BG edition, added corrections, fingerings, and other markings, and sent them to Universal Edition to serve as the printer's text. The upper right corner of the first page bears the publisher's stamp (dated May 14, 1910) indicating that the pages were ready to be set: "14-5-10 / 'Universal-Edition' A.-G. / WIEN / Zum Stich!" (Schenker's Preface is dated September 1909, but the work did not appear in print until 1910.) There are markings in blue pencil, probably made by an editor, that change the format of the heading at the top of the page and the footnote at the bottom to conform with what was to appear in the Universal Edition print. (Some additional changes, such as the respelling of "Fantasie" as "Phantasie," are not marked.) The plate number of the BG edition is crossed out in blue pencil and is replaced by the plate number of Schenker's edition: U.E. 2540. Thus Schenker's statement that the BG edition served as "the chief source for the present edition" may be taken quite literally.

Schenker's own markings include fingerings, footnotes (giving the realization of ornaments), dynamic markings, symbols indicating where the realization of the arpeggio sections should be inserted, and alterations of certain notes or accidentals. (The specific changes Schenker made in the text of the BG edition will be noted below as they occur.) Except for the first two fingering numbers, which are entered in red ink, all the fingerings are written in pencil, as are most of the other indications. The printed slurs, ties, and phrase marks are left untouched (though a few slurs found in the BG edition appear to have been inadvertently omitted). Bar numbers are added in green or blue pencil every five measures. Another set of numbers is entered at the end of every bar that corresponds to the last bar of a system or page in the final Universal Edition print; these may have been added later as an aid to checking this copy with the proof.

The markings that Schenker entered into this copy do not entirely conform to the final version given in the Universal Edition print; he must have made additional changes (especially in the fingerings and dynamic markings) at some later stage in the publication process. Thus, while this document provides a fascinating glimpse into the evolution of the present work, the markings it contains are obviously superseded by those in the printed edition.

Schenker's entries in his copy of the BG edition provide a possible explanation for the discrepancy between his statement in the Preface—that along with the editorial *crescendo* and *diminuendo* signs, the Fantasy contains some added dynamic indications in parentheses—and the fact that no signs in parentheses are present in the printed edition. This omission is unusual, since Schenker attached great importance to the differentiation of editorial additions from original markings—see, for example, the quotations given in note 112 below, from *Ein Beitrag zur Ornamentik*, p. 13 (English translation, pp. 31-32 and footnote 17; see Appendix: Works of Heinrich Schenker). In Schenker's own copy of the BG edition, the only pencilled dynamic markings found in the Fantasy are the *crescendo* and *diminuendo* signs; there are in fact no added indications such as *f* or *p*. In the Fugue, however, where the BG edition has no printed dynamic markings, Schenker pencilled in his own, and placed all of the *forte* and *piano* indications in parentheses. However, he must have later asked the printer to ignore his parentheses, preferring instead to inform the reader that all of the indications in the Fugue were his own (see his Preface). At some later stage, he added further dynamic markings to the Fantasy; the final Universal Edition print contains the following dynamic indications that are not found in the BG edition:

bar 9	*mf*
bar 13	*f*
bar 15	*f*
bar 21	*mf*
bar 26	*f*
bar 27	*f*

However, they are not differentiated in any way. Schenker probably placed them in parentheses (remarking on this in his Preface), only to have them ignored by the printer along with those in the Fugue. (Even the BG edition's *printed* parentheses around the *f* in bar 58 of the Fantasy were excised.)

There is another discrepancy between dynamic markings in the BG edition and the Universal Edition print: a *p* in bar 77 and an *f* in bar 78 of the Fantasy, present as printed signs in the BG edition, are missing in Schenker's edition. This omission was probably due to an oversight, which it is now possible to rectify in the score that accompanies this translation (see note 62 below).

Also part of the Oster Collection is Schenker's own copy of the Röntgen edition of the Chromatic Fantasy and Fugue, which had been issued by Universal Edition around the turn of the century, several years before the publication of Schenker's edition. This copy, too, contains detailed indications in Schenker's hand. They are written with great care—none are in pencil; instead, red or black ink is used for the added notes, fingerings, dynamic markings, phrase marks, and symbols designating inserted arpeggio realizations (the symbols are the same as those found in the BG copy). These corrections are sometimes entered over the printed version, which has been scraped away. In the main, the fingerings correspond to those given in the BG copy, as do many of the dynamic markings. However, no printer's marks are to be found on any of the pages. It is possible that Schenker originally intended to use these pages as the printer's text—Ernst Oster remarks in his listing: "vielleicht Schenkers Stichvorlage"—but that he later decided to use the less cluttered BG edition instead. (As Röntgen explains in his preface, his text, though based on the BG edition, does contain editorial additions.) Schenker's entries in his copies of both the BG and the Röntgen editions seem to reflect the same stage in the editorial process; neither copy contains all of the features of the final Universal Edition print.]

[2. The present edition, unlike Schenker's *Erläuterungsausgabe* of the late Beethoven sonatas (see Appendix: Works of Heinrich Schenker), does not include a detailed study of the manuscript sources, probably because the autograph was not available. Ernst Naumann lists the manuscripts and prints that served as sources for the BG edition (pp. xl-xlii); an expanded and regrouped listing of extant sources is given by Georg von Dadelsen and Klaus Rönnau in the commentary to their edition of the Chromatic Fantasy and Fugue: J. S. Bach, *Fantasien, Präludien und Fugen* (Munich: G. Henle, 1973), pp. 133-35 (hereafter referred to as the Henle edition). Hans T. David, in his first major article, "Die Gestalt von Bachs Chromatischer Fantasie," *Bach Jahrbuch*, vol. 23 (1926), included a detailed philological study of the sources (pp. 56-64) supplemented by a chart relating the manuscript copies to three hypothetical autograph versions (p. 59).

The dynamic markings given in the BG edition (and reproduced by Schenker) are found in a manuscript copy of the Fantasy which Naumann regarded as reliable (Berlin, Stiftung Preussischer Kulturbesitz, Mus.ms.Bach P 577). However, Dadelsen and Rönnau consider the dynamic indications given in this copy to be spurious, as did David.]

[3. Schenker had enumerated these editions in a list of abbreviations that preceded his text. In this translation they will be referred to by the name of each editor (or publisher) as follows:

Bischoff — J. S. Bach, *Clavierwerke*, ed. by Hans Bischoff (Berlin: Steingräber, 1880-88), vol. 1, pp. 110-22. The translation used in subsequent quotations from Bischoff's footnotes is by Alexander Lipsky, found in the reprint: J. S. Bach, *Chromatic Fantasy and Fugue* (New York: Kalmus, 1942).

Bülow — J. S. Bach, *Oeuvres choisis pour le piano*, no. 5: *Fantasie Chromatique* . . ., ed. by Hans von Bülow (Berlin: Bote & Bock,

1859-65). This edition has been reprinted by many publishers, including G. Schirmer in New York.

Busoni   J. S. Bach, *Chromatische Fantasie und Fuge*, ed. by Ferruccio Busoni (Berlin: N. Simrock, 1902). This edition was reprinted in J. S. Bach, *Klavierwerke* (Leipzig: Breitkopf & Härtel, 1915), vol. 14, pp. 1-30, together with the BG edition's reading of the Fantasy and the text of the Rust variant (see note 12 below).

Peters   J. S. Bach, *Klavierwerke*, ed. by Adolf Ruthardt (Leipzig: C. F. Peters, 1894), vol. 10, Peters Edition no. 3514, pp. 20-35, and pp. 49-55 (variants I and II). As Ruthardt states in his preface, "the text of this edition is absolutely identical with the old edition of Czerny, Griepenkerl and Roitzsch": J. S. Bach, *Klavierwerke* (Leipzig: C. F. Peters, 1868-80), vol. 10, Peters Edition no. 207, pp. 20-31 and Anhang; Ruthardt changed only the phrase marks and fingering. Though Schenker specifically cites the Ruthardt edition in his list, he must have consulted the earlier Peters edition as well; his text includes a reference to its preface. This preface stems from F. K. Griepenkerl's edition of 1819, also published by Peters, which bore the following subtitle: "Neue Ausgabe mit einer Bezeichnung ihres wahren Vortrags, wie derselbe von J. S. Bach auf Friedemann, von diesem auf Forkel und von Forkel auf seine Schüler gekommen." This statement by Griepenkerl, a student of Forkel, can be traced to Forkel's assertion, in his monograph on Bach (1802), that he received an autograph of the Chromatic Fantasy and Fugue from Wilhelm Friedemann; see *The Bach Reader*, ed. by Hans T. David and Arthur Mendel (revised ed.; New York: Norton, 1966), p. 342. Forkel's manuscript copy (Berlin, Stiftung Preussischer Kulturbesitz, Mus.ms.Bach P 212) is thought to have been based on this autograph. A copy of Forkel's manuscript (Berlin, Stiftung Preussischer Kulturbesitz, Mus.ms.Bach P 1083) served as the basis for the first edition (Vienna: Hoffmeister; Leipzig: Bureau de Musique de C. F. Peters, 1803), publisher's plate no. 74; this print gave rise to subsequent editions published by Peters. See Dadelsen and Rönnau's commentary to the Henle edition, pp. 134-35, and David, "Die Gestalt von Bachs Chromatischer Fantasie," pp. 56-65.

Reinecke   J. S. Bach, *Klavierwerke*, ed. by Carl Reinecke (Leipzig: Breitkopf & Härtel, 1871-83), vol. 7, pp. 48-59.

Röntgen   J. S. Bach, *Chromatische Fantasie und Fuge*, ed. by Julius Röntgen (Vienna: Universal Edition, ca. 1900), Universal Edition no. 520. See note 1 above.

These editions fall into two basic groups. The first group comprises those whose text is derived from that of the BG edition—the Busoni and Röntgen editions. The Bischoff edition can be included in this group; it antedates the BG edition but

Bischoff consulted many of the same sources as Naumann. The editions of the second group—those of Bülow and Reinecke and the various editions published by Peters—stem from the reading given in Forkel's manuscript copy, which Naumann regards as a variant (see his preface, pp. xli-xliii).]

*4. The Handel Society in London.

[5. The entire text of this letter (to Ignaz Moscheles in London) is given in Felix Mendelssohn Bartholdy, *Briefe*, vol. 2: *Briefe aus den Jahren 1833 bis 1847*, ed. by Paul and Carl Mendelssohn Bartholdy (Leipzig: Hermann Mendelssohn, 1864), pp. 38-41. It was written in the year preceding the publication of Mendelssohn's edition of *Israel in Egypt* by the Handel Society; Moscheles and George A. Macfarren were members of the Society's council. The edition of the *Coronation Anthems* mentioned in the letter had been published by the Society in 1844. The translation used here is by Ignaz Moscheles's son Felix Moscheles, as given in *Letters of Felix Mendelssohn to Ignaz and Charlotte Moscheles* (London: Trübner, 1888), pp. 251-52. The translation has been slightly emended. Here, as elsewhere, italics have been used to represent the widely spaced type of the original German.]

[6. Johannes Brahms, *Briefwechsel*, vol. 3: *Johannes Brahms im Briefwechsel mit Karl Reinthaler, Max Bruch, Hermann Deiters, Friedr. Heimsoeth, Karl Reinecke, Ernst Rudorff, Bernhard und Luise Scholz*, ed. by Wilhelm Altmann (2nd ed.; Berlin: Deutsche Brahms-Gesellschaft, 1912), pp. 172-73. The letter concerns problems that arose during the preparation of the Breitkopf & Härtel *Gesamtausgabe* of Chopin's works, whose editors included Brahms, Ernst Rudorff, and Woldemar Bargiel. Brahms is replying to questions posed by Rudorff in a letter dated October 21, 1877. (See Brahms, *Briefwechsel*, vol. 3, pp. 168-71.)

Brahms's letter is also cited by Oswald Jonas in his article "On the Study of Chopin's Manuscripts," *Chopin-Jahrbuch 1956*, pp. 142-44; wherever the excerpts presented by him and by Schenker coincide, Jonas's translation is used here. The original German reads as follows (a few minor errors in the examples as given in the *Briefwechsel* have been tacitly corrected; in numbering the bars, the Ballade's incomplete opening measure has been considered bar 1):

Hier möchte ich so ausführlich wie dort bescheiden sein. . . . In der *a* moll-"Ballade" würde ich die auch mir unverständliche

Example A

bar 46

doch stehen lassen. Auch dies *A*,

Example B

bar 54

welches zudem mit dem spätern

Example C

bar 148

einigermassen korrespondiert. Für die 3 Quinten

Example D

bars 114–115

aber bin ich am entschiedensten! . . . Sehr wünschte ich, Bargiel wäre mit uns eins, dass wir nicht versuchen Chopins Orthographie verbessern zu wollen! Es wäre nur ein kleiner Schritt, auch seinen Satz anzugreifen.

Brahms is discussing the Ballade, op. 38 (known as the *F*-major Ballade because of its opening, but always correctly referred to by Brahms as the *A*-minor Ballade). His first musical example (example A) cites the rhythmic notation given for the repeated a^1s at the end of bar 46; the notation of this bar is the subject of another article by Jonas, "Ein textkritisches Problem in der Ballade op. 38 von Frédéric Chopin," *Acta Musicologica*, vol. 35 (1963), pp. 155-58. In addition to presenting the relevant portions of both Rudorff's and Brahms's letters, Jonas transcribes two letters from Schenker's correspondence that were in his possession. They date from 1908, a year before the completion of Schenker's edition of the Chromatic Fantasy and Fugue. The first is a letter Schenker wrote to Rudorff (who was by then a very old man) and the second is Rudorff's reply; both letters concern the solution to the puzzle of this bar in the Chopin Ballade. Jonas himself adds a convincing contribution. Rudorff, Schenker, and Jonas all agree with Brahms that Chopin's original notation—a single triplet indication for the six notes—should be maintained.

The letters transcribed by Jonas also show that Schenker and Rudorff exchanged views on the value of consulting original sources; Schenker's words reinforce the opinion he expresses in the present text: "This example provides further evidence that one should always remain true to the original in every instance, and I am pleased to find substantiation in these letters . . . that Brahms was steadfast in his fidelity to the original."

Brahms's letter to Rudorff cited by Schenker in the present work contains further musical examples from the Ballade. The next two are from bar 54 and bar 148 (examples B and C; both give only the left-hand part, with the doubling octaves omitted). Here Brahms is replying directly to a question posed by Rudorff, who had asked if the *A* in bar 54 should perhaps be changed to *c*. Brahms's reply that the *A* should be retained because of the correspondence of this bar with bar 148 seems to be related to the fact that both measures directly precede the restatement of the opening motive of the *Presto con fuoco* section—in each case the motive is introduced by three descending notes in the bass: *B♭-A-G* in bars 54-55 and *c-B♮-A* in bars 148-149. Thus Brahms may have felt that Rudorff's suggested change, *c-B♭-A-G* instead of *A-B♭-A-G*, would obscure the correspondence of the passages, since the use of the passing tone *c* would cause the three-note descent in the first example to become part of a larger line.

The last example in Brahms's letter cites the fifths found in bars 114-115 (example D). Such examples were always of great interest to Brahms; see Paul Mast, "Brahms's Study, Octaven u. Quinten u. A., with Schenker's Commentary Translated," pp. 1-196. (See Appendix: Works of Heinrich Schenker.) This example, however, is not included in that study.]

*7. Cf., for example, Mozart's Fantasy in *C* minor, K. 396.

*8. As, for example, in the Toccatas in *D* major and *G* minor [*BWV* 912 and *BWV* 915].

[9. *Teiler.* This is one of Schenker's earliest uses of a term that was to assume great importance in his later writings. Here it designates a dominant chord that closes off a segment in the design or form of a composition.]

*10. Spitta, vol. 2, pp. 661-62. [See these pages in Philipp Spitta, *Johann Sebastian Bach* (Wiesbaden: Brietkopf & Härtel, 1979; reprinted from the 4th ed. of 1930). The translation used here, slightly altered, is by Clara Bell and J. A. Fuller-Maitland (New York: Dover, 1952; reprinted from the Novello ed. of 1889), vol. 3, pp. 181-82. Regarding the earlier version of the Chromatic Fantasy cited by Spitta, see note 12 below. Spitta's reference to the "earlier Fantasy in *D* major" is to the Toccata, *BWV* 912, mentioned by Schenker in note 8 above.]

*11. Cf. the equally erroneous rendition of the original thirty-second and sixty-fourth notes given at the beginning of Tausig's arrangement of Bach's Organ Toccata in *D* minor. [Schenker's own copy of this piano arrangement of *BWV* 565, Carl Tausig, *Bearbeitung für den Konzertvortrag; Toccata und Fuge (D moll) für die Orgel (Pedal & Manual) von Joh. Seb. Bach* (Berlin: Schlesinger, 1902), is part of the Oster Collection. Schenker's copy contains many of his own performance indications—fingerings, dynamic markings, tempo indications, and pedal signs, as well as some corrections of Tausig's readings. These include the correction of Tausig's five uniform sixty-fourth notes to the original four sixty-fourth notes followed by a thirty-second note (bar 1, second eighth).]

*12. The Rust version [*BWV* 903a] may be found in the BG edition [pp. 219-20] and in the Peters edition (variant I) [pp. 49-52. This version provides a substantially different reading for bars 1-20 of the Fantasy (though the first two measures are essentially the same). The BG edition presents only the divergent section, the opening 23 bars. Schenker, however, follows the Peters edition in printing the entire Fantasy according to the Rust version (see the variant presented at the end of the score that accompanies this translation). He adds repeat signs at bars 3 and 23, for which he is criticized by David ("Die Gestalt von Bachs Chromatischer Fantasie," p. 58, footnote 2). For further discussion of the Rust manuscript, see Spitta, *Johann*

Sebastian Bach, vol. 2, pp. 841-43 (English translation, vol. 3, pp. 291-92); David, pp. 57-61; and the Henle edition, p. 134.]

*13. C.P.E. Bach, *Versuch über die wahre Art das Clavier zu spielen*, Part II, chapter 41, §12; see also §13 of this same chapter for more specific details. [See the facsimile of the editions of 1753 (Part I) and 1762 (Part II), ed. by Lothar Hoffman-Erbrecht (2nd ed.; Leipzig: Breitkopf & Härtel, 1969), Part II, pp. 336-39. Here, and in all further citations from this work, the English translation is from C.P.E. Bach, *Essay on the True Art of Playing Keyboard Instruments*, translated and ed. by William J. Mitchell (New York: Norton, 1949). §12 and §13 are found on pp. 438-40.

Schenker provides a detailed commentary on this chapter of the *Versuch* in his essay, "Die Kunst der Improvisation," *Das Meisterwerk in der Musik, Jahrbuch* I, pp. 11-40; see p. 16 ff. See Appendix: Works of Heinrich Schenker.]

[14. In his own copy of the BG edition (the printer's text for the present edition), Schenker crossed out the natural sign that is printed in parentheses above the bb^1, thereby offering a definitive reading for a point left undecided by Naumann. (He had listed bar 5 in the discussion of the BG source in his introduction.)]

[15. *Auskomponiert*. In the present study, the term *Auskomponierung* (composing-out) generally means the spreading out over a considerable stretch of time (and therefore the horizontalization) of a conceptually vertical sonority—a chord or, as here, an interval. Examples of this kind of composing-out are especially plentiful in a piece such as the Chromatic Fantasy. In a certain sense this usage is related to Schenker's later theory of structural levels: the vertical harmony (i.e., the *Stufe* or scale-step) represents the deeper level of structure, to be composed out on the surface of the composition. See also Oswald Jonas, *Introduction to the Theory of Heinrich Schenker*, translated and ed. by John Rothgeb (New York: Longman, 1982), p. 37 ff.]

[16. Busoni places an accent (-) over bb^1 (first quarter, third sixteenth) and bb^1 (second quarter, fifth sixteenth) in bar 7, as well as in the analogous points in bar 9: over f^1 (first quarter, third sixteenth) and $f\sharp^1$ (second quarter, fifth sixteenth).]

[17. Bischoff's edition has eb^1; his footnote reads as follows: "Bülow has E instead of Eb . . .; however, this is not authentic."]

*18. See the preface to the BG edition, p. xliii.

*19. Cf. Schenker, *Harmonielehre*, §166 [pp. 407-9 (English translation, pp. 309-10)] and also figure 235 [on p. 267 (English translation, example 174 on p. 204). See Appendix: Works of Heinrich Schenker.

In §166, under the heading "Various Forms of Suspension," Schenker states that in free composition a suspension "can be resolved by upward or downward progression" and "may be prepared or may set in freely, without preparation." The example he cites, like example 5 of the present study, contains suspensions that enter freely and resolve upwards. See also Jonas, *Introduction to the Theory of Heinrich Schenker*, translated and ed. by John Rothgeb, pp. 94-95, footnote 58; and Schenker, "A Contribution to the Study of Ornamentation," translated by Hedi Siegel, p. 54, footnote 4 (see Appendix: Works of Heinrich Schenker).]

[20. An octave higher in the fourth quarter: f^2-$g\sharp^2$-a^2.]

*21. Schenker, *Harmonielehre*, §142 and §162 [pp. 356-59 and pp. 398-99 (English translation, pp. 268-71 and pp. 300-301). Later, Schenker characterized the $G\sharp$-$B\natural$-D-F as a neighboring sonority; in his personal copy of the Universal Edition print of the present study (see the Translator's Foreword) he wrote "nbhm [Nebennoten-harmonie]" in the margin at this point in the text. At the beginning of bar 17 of the score, he wrote "nbh" and beneath it "=$\sharp$IV$_{\natural 3}^{7}$." The note names "*a-gis-a*" (*a-g$\sharp$-a*) over "V—" are found below these indications.]

*22. Cf. Schenker, *Harmonielehre*, figures 148, 150, 155, etc. [on pp. 185, 186, and 189 (English translation, examples 114, 116, and 121 on pp. 142, 143, and 146)—further illustrations of passing sonorities].

[23. The number 3 in parentheses appearing at the beginning and end of this series of numbers signifies the sixteenth-note position of two hypothetical statements of the five-note motive, one preceding the first actual statement and the other following the last. The hypothetical statements of the motive would have started on the third sixteenth of the last quarter in bar 18 and on the third sixteenth of the first quarter in bar 20. The double line appears at the place where the series could begin again in the same rhythmic location, thus closing the "circle."]

*24. After Bach, hardly any composer manifested this rhythmic technique in such perfection—except Brahms. [Schenker's personal copy contains annotations in the margin at this point in the text (possibly written in the hand of his wife) and at the bottom of the page (unmistakably in Schenker's hand) that cite two specific examples of Brahms's use of this technique. The first is the opening of the Intermezzo, op. 119, no. 3 (not no. 2, as the marginal note has it), characterized as a "four-note motive whose rhythmic placement is changed at each of its four repetitions" and illustrated as in example E.

Example E

bar 1

The second example is from the Rhapsody in *B* minor, op. 79, no. 1, bars 84-86. Schenker illustrates the changing position of the repeated motive with respect to the four quarters of each bar (example F).]

Example F

bars 84–86

79

*25. Bischoff offers the following annotations: "The frequent deviations in the manuscripts in respect to the descending minor scale are well known, particularly in regard to the sixth and seventh degrees of the scale. This is especially true in this composition." It is obvious that Bischoff's comment in no way settles our question.

*26. Cf. the $c\natural^1$ in bar 17, which is likewise a partial expression of a chord arising during the composing-out process. [Schenker's term *Teilharmonie* will elsewhere be rendered as "chordal fragment."]

[27. Schenker reprints the ornament given in the BG edition; in calling it a *Pralltriller* instead of a mordent he seems to be characterizing its length rather than its direction. For Schenker's discussion of the *Pralltriller*, see *Ein Beitrag zur Ornamentik*, pp. 40-41 (English translation, pp. 82-84).]

[28. Example 8 closely resembles the variant given by Bischoff.]

*29. Cf., for example, chapter 31 of C.P.E. Bach, *Versuch über die wahre Art das Clavier zu spielen* [Part II, pp. 266-68 (English translation, pp. 384-86, "The Fermata")], or chapter 15 of J. J. Quantz, *Versuch einer Anweisung die Flöte traversiere zu spielen* [facsimile of the edition of 1789, edited by Hans-Peter Schmitz (Kassel: Bärenreiter, 1953), pp. 151-64; English translation by Edward R. Reilly, *On Playing the Flute* (London: Faber & Faber; New York: Schirmer, 1966), pp. 179-95, "Of Cadenzas"].

[30. In Bülow's edition the trill takes up an entire measure, which is inserted between bars 20 and 21.]

*31. Cf. my remarks on bar 19. [In "Die Kunst der Improvisation," *Meisterwerk*, I, p. 21, Schenker refers to the Chromatic Fantasy; he relates bars 21, 22, and 31 to an example from C.P.E. Bach's *Versuch*, Part II, chapter 41, §13 (not §14 as Schenker has it), pp. 338-39, figure g (English translation, pp. 440-41, figure 478g). This example demonstrates the avoidance of the augmented second when arpeggiating a diminished seventh chord. The markings in Schenker's personal copy of the present work reflect this thought: at bar 21 of the score we find the annotations "verm [inderter] drkg [Dreiklang] *b-g-e*" (diminished triad *b♭-g-e*); "*e cis b* [?] vermieden" (*e-c♯-b♭* avoided). At bar 31, second quarter, Schenker places a cross between the $c\sharp^2$ and the g^1 and writes: "vermied[ener] Raum *b* [?] *cis*" (avoided interval *b♭-c♯*). In addition, the score contains markings that clarify the rhythmic organization of bars 21-22: Schenker uses phrase marks to indicate the three groups of six thirty-second notes and marks off each larger group of three chord-tones with a vertical line.]

*32. Given, for example, in the Peters edition [as variant II, p. 53—the basis for Schenker's example 9; a slightly different version is found in the preface to the BG edition, p. xliii. David, in "Die Gestalt von Bachs Chromatischer Fantasie," pp. 59-61, links the manuscript source for this variant (Berlin, Deutsche Staatsbibliothek, Mus.ms.Bach P 803) to one of the earlier, no longer extant, autograph versions. See also the commentary to the Henle edition, p. 134.]

[33. In the BG and some other editions, the sharp is placed in parentheses and is printed above the f^1. In his own copy of the BG edition (the printer's text for the present edition), Schenker crossed out this sharp and replaced it with a sharp written in front of the note. (He had included bar 25 in the list of alterations given in his introduction.) The Henle edition reads this note as $f\natural^1$.]

*34. Cf. the commentary to bars 17 and 19.

*35. The same is true, moreover, of the technique of so-called continuo playing.

*36. Cf. C.P.E. Bach, *Versuch*, Part II, chapter 41, §13 [pp. 337-39 (English translation, pp. 439-40); see also note 13 above].

[37. Reference to other examples of written-out arpeggios is made in Schenker's personal copy at this point. These include Beethoven, Sonata in *C* major, op. 2, no. 3, first movement (see bars 97-108) and J. S. Bach, Concerto in *D* minor for harpsichord, *BWV* 1052, first movement. For the latter example, Schenker cites vol. 17, pp. 16-17, of the Bach-Gesellschaft edition (where bars 166-171 contain a written-out arpeggio figure) as well as the Anhang, which presents an earlier version of the Concerto (the same arpeggio is given as a series of chords on p. 289).]

*38. [*BWV* 894] Peters Edition no. 211. [J. S. Bach, *Klavierwerke*, ed. by C. Czerny, F. K. Griepenkerl, and F. A. Roitzch (Leipzig: C. F. Peters, 1868-80), vol. 14, pp. 14-27]; BG edition, vol. 36 [pp. 91-103, bars 77-85 of the Prelude].

*39. To facilitate reference to the ensuing analysis, I have numbered each chord but have otherwise faithfully reproduced the rhythmic division of the original. [Schenker gives corresponding numbers to Bach's arpeggiated figures (example 13), and in his discussion he refers to the figures by number. Each figure consists of two arpeggiations and extends from the third quarter of one bar through the second quarter of the next. Schenker marked the same figure numbers in his own copy of the BG edition that contains this Prelude (vol. 36; see note 1 above). He must have been working from that copy when he wrote this section of the present study, for he made indications that correspond entirely with his discussion in the text. These indications have been reproduced in example 13, with the abbreviations interpreted as follows: "h" signifies "harmonischer Ton," rendered in the text as "chord tone"; "W" signifies "Wechselnote," translated in the text as "accented passing tone."]

[40. Here Schenker uses the term *acciaccatura* in C.P.E. Bach's meaning. The following description, illustrated by several examples, is found in the *Versuch*, Part II, chapter 41, §13, pp. 337-39 (English translation, pp. 439-40): "In the interests of elegance the major or minor second may be struck and quitted below each tone of a broken triad or a relationship based on a triad. This is called "breaking with *acciaccature*."]

*41. Concerning this point, see Schenker, *Kontrapunkt*, I, §6 [pp. 306-8. (See Appendix: Works of Heinrich Schenker.) In this section of *Kontrapunkt* Schenker discusses the "faulty leap of a third," which is to be avoided in two-voice third species writing. In giving a related example from free composition, Schenker cites the last two quarters of bar 80 and the first three quarters of bar 81 of this same Prelude (i.e., the entire fourth figure and the beginning of the fifth figure); he offers the same explanation as that given here for Bach's use of d^1 rather than b in bar 81.]

[42. As Schenker's markings show, the same is true of the *b* in the eighth figure (see example 13, bar 84, the last two thirty-second note groups.]

*43. Cf. Schenker, *Harmonielehre*, figure 151 [on p. 186 (English translation, example 117 on p. 143)].

[44. As an aid to the expression of these connections in performance, Schenker marked them in his own copy of Tausig's arrangement (see note 11 above). He drew a long arrow in red pencil through bars 22-27, connecting the chords that are given here in example 21a. Another long red arrow connects the chords found eleven and seven bars before the end, the last two chords given in example 21b. (Schenker seems to have miscounted the eleventh bar before the end as the tenth; the first four bar numbers he gives in example 21b have therefore been corrected.)]

*45. This "harmonic" scheme, as well as that given for bar 49 ff., is still based on the ideas expressed in *Harmonielehre*, which appeared just three years before the present study. Had this study been written later, surely Schenker would instead have called attention to the motion of the upper voice: eb^2-d^2-c^2-$b\natural^1$ (!) in bars 33-34 had to be transformed by Bach into eb^2-$(c\sharp^2)$-d^2-$c\natural^2$-bb^1 (!) [in bars 38-41] in order to reach the bb^1 that begins the "concealed melodic line" [referred to in Schenker's discussion] of the recitative starting in bar 49. (Jonas)

[A slightly later stage of Schenker's thinking is reflected in the annotations he made in his personal copy. He made corrections and additions to the scheme given in example 23: the $B\natural$ indicated at bar 34 is placed in parentheses and the Eb given at bar 40 is labeled "dg [Durchgang]" (passing tone). A reinterpretation is given in the margin:

$$A\text{-}F\text{-}D$$
A major / IV-V-I - IV♯-V-I

(The series of Roman numerals was extended to bar 49 by the addition of ♯I-II-V.) These changes are reflected in a sketch of bars 33-49 found in the score (example G).

Example G

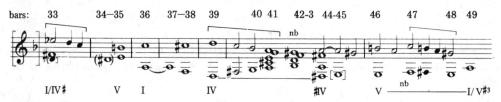

The first five bass tones of the sketch are also pencilled into bars 33-37 of the score. The bass tones, as well as other features of the sketch, suggest the existence of elisions and replacements.]

[46. In Schenker's personal copy, a sketch of the lower voices of bars 49-63 that provides a broader organization for the scheme given in example 24 is found in the score (see example H).]

Example H

*47. The "line" (*Urlinie*), an idea Schenker developed later, is already evident here. One might also mention the "initial ascent" (*Anstieg*) to the important note bb^2: d^2-e^2 (bar 1) to f^2 (bar 2) to f^2-g^2-a^2-bb^2 (bar 3); see also bars 27-30. (Jonas)

[A sketch that incorporates the same "line" as that given in example 25 is found in Schenker's personal copy (see example I).

Example I

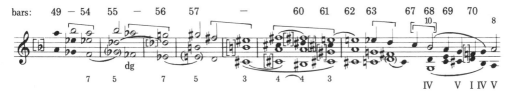

Among the papers in the Oster Collection are several loose sheets containing fragmentary graphs of the Chromatic Fantasy and Fugue. These include a sketch of the opening of the Fantasy (see example J), which in some ways corresponds to Jonas's remarks on the initial ascent.]

Example J

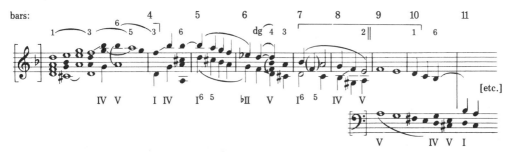

*48. In some editions (e.g., the Peters edition) these rhythmically altered recitative openings are presented as variant readings, but in others (e.g., the Bülow and Reinecke editions) they are unfortunately incorporated into the text itself.

*49. Cf. the preface to the Peters edition [specifically the following passage: "Each recitative statement has been notated with a shortened initial note—not falsely to suggest a dotted and distorted rendition, but only to indicate that each statement

begins with an upbeat and that the accent should thus be placed on the second note."
The reference is to the edition of Czerny, Griepenkerl, and Roitzsch; see note 3 above.]

*50. An explanation for how the ominous double flat found its way into a large
number of manuscript copies of the Fantasy may lie in the old way of writing the
double flat as a single, enlarged flat. Misinterpretations can easily arise from this
older notational practice, since the size of handwritten accidentals is always relative.
(Jonas)

[The reading of bar 50 given in example 27 is the one preferred by most scholars
and editors. (Modern authentic editions tend to substitute $a\natural^1$ for $b\flat\flat^1$, among them
the Henle edition.) A lengthy defense of this version is given in Ludwig Czaczkes,
Bachs Chromatische Fantasie und Fuge (Vienna: Österreichischer Bundesverlag für
Unterricht, Wissenschaft und Kunst, 1971), pp. 39-46; it is also discussed in
Hermann Keller, *Die Klavierwerke Bachs* (Leipzig: C. F. Peters, 1950), pp. 159-60.
Spitta and David favor the $b\flat\flat^1$; see Spitta, *Johann Sebastian Bach*, vol. 2, pp. 841-43
(English translation, vol. 3, pp. 291-92); and David, "Die Gestalt von Bachs
Chromatischer Fantasie," appendix of musical examples, pp. 8-9 (examples 18 and
21) and p. 20 (footnote 10). The same reading (with $b\flat\flat^1$) is given in the BG edition,
with which Schenker was in disagreement. (This was one of his departures from the
BG edition that he had listed in his introduction.) Schenker, instead, followed the
Peters edition—Griepenkerl's transmission of the reading found in Forkel's manuscript copy (see note 3 above).

In preparing his own copy of the BG edition for use as the printer's text, Schenker
wrote his substitute for the printed bar 50 at the bottom of the page, adding the
remark "Fussnote!" (though no footnote appears in his edition at this point). In his
copy of the Röntgen edition, perhaps originally intended as the printer's text (see
note 1 above), his correction is pasted over the printed measure.]

[51. That is, the diminished chord.]

*52. Cf. Schenker, *Harmonielehre*, §108 [pp. 250-51 (English translation, pp.
190-92)].

*53. Cf. Schenker, *Harmonielehre*, §34 and §64 [pp. 100-103 and pp. 162-64
(English translation, pp. 79-81 and pp. 126-27); both sections contain some discussion of enharmonic equivalence].

*54. In Liszt's transcription. [The reference is to the Prelude (Fantasia) of the
"Great" Fugue in *G* minor, *BWV* 542. See J. S. Bach, *Orgelfantasie und Fuge in
G-moll*, transcribed by Franz Liszt (Berlin: M. Bahn, 1870).]

*55. Cf. Schenker, *Ein Beitrag zur Ornamentik*, p. 36, footnote 4, figure 20!
[(English translation, pp. 74-75, footnote 33, example H), where a similar trill in
Bach's English Suite no. 6 is discussed].

*56. Cf. Schenker, *Ein Beitrag zur Ornamentik*, p. 36, §6 [(English translation,
pp. 76-79). In this section, which is entitled "The Trill at a Dotted Note," Schenker
discusses the need for such a separation (*Zwischenraum*) and presents a durational
diagram of the trill's components.]

[57. Schenker provides much the same realization in the score, as a footnote to bar 62. In his own copy of the BG edition, the realization is entered as a pencilled footnote, in exactly the same form as that given in example 28 (i.e., with the grace note written as a thirty-second note).]

[58. The fully written-out form of this trill is given in a footnote to bar 67 of the score; in Schenker's personal copy the fingering 4 5 3 5 [3] 2 4 5 4 is added.]

[59. See the end of the commentary to bar 11.]

*60. The variants either replace the original figures, as in the Bülow and Reinecke editions, or are placed above the original text and are thus clearly identified as variants (this is done in the Bischoff and Peters editions). [Schenker probably based his example 31 on the variant readings given in the Peters edition (Griepenkerl's rendition of Forkel's version). In his discussion, Schenker refers to the individual figures by number; these numbers have been added to example 31.]

*61. Cf. C.P.E. Bach, *Versuch*, Part I, chapter 2, section 9 [pp. 112-14 (English translation, pp. 143-46); see especially §4]. See also Schenker, *Ein Beitrag zur Ornamentik*, p. 23 [English translation, pp. 48-49].

[62. At this point in the score of his personal copy, Schenker added the dynamic signs *p* and *f* at the fourth quarter of bar 77 and the first quarter of bar 78, respectively. The symbols are large and written heavily in red pencil; they are also indicated in the right margin, as if correcting proof. Schenker clearly regarded their omission from his edition as an error. They appear as printed dynamic signs in the BG edition— and thus in the printer's text for the present edition—but their omission seems to have slipped by unnoticed until the work appeared in print. They have been included in the score that accompanies this translation.]

[63. Schenker is alluding to Griepenkerl's subtitle and preface to the Peters edition of 1819 (see note 3 above). See also Dadelsen and Rönnau's commentary to the Henle edition, pp. 134-35.]

[64. *Die aus Schlussgründen zu überwindende Mitte*.]

*65. To be discussed later. [See the end of the commentary to bar 131.]

[66. One such edition is Bernardus Boekelman's *Eight Fugues from J. S. Bach's Well-Tempered Clavichord*, with analytical expositions in colors and appended harmonic schemes (London: Novello, Ewer, & Co., 1895, 1912), also issued by other publishers in Amsterdam, Leipzig, Milan, and Paris.]

*67. Cf. the following example (example K) in the supplementary volume to Schenker, *Der freie Satz*, [figure 20, 2 (see Appendix: Works of Heinrich Schenker)]:

Example K

J.S. Bach, Chromatic Fantasy and Fugue

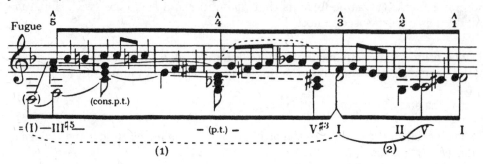

Cf. also Schenker's essay, "Das Organische der Fuge," *Meisterwerk*, II. (Jonas)

[The graph of the opening of the Fugue given in *Der freie Satz* is described in §78 of the text, on pp. 68-69 (English translation, p. 34), under the heading "The Combination of an Unprolonged Fundamental Line with Two Bass Arpeggiations," as follows: "The beginning of the Fugue is preceded by a Fantasy, which expresses the I, so that the fugue subject can enter on III in the middle of the first bass arpeggiation." Several details of this graph are discussed in other sections of *Der freie Satz*: The consonant inner-voice passing tones e^1 and g^1, supported by c^1 in bar 2, are shown to have originated as dissonant passing tones above the bass tone f; see §170, pp. 103-4 (English translation, p. 61). The stationary boundary tone g^1 in bars 4-5 is referred to in §260, p. 161 (English translation, p. 104). The first bass arpeggiation, I-III$^{♮5}$-V$^{♯3}$, is cited as an example of a progression in minor that produces conflicting chromatic tones in the foreground; see §248, p. 142 (English translation, p. 91) and figure 113, 2.

Perhaps most significant are Schenker's comments regarding the representation of the bass in the graph of a fugal subject; see §243, pp. 136-37 (English translation, p. 88). In presenting examples that show the transference of forms of the fundamental structure to the foreground, Schenker makes the following important statement (in his discussion of figure 109e): "Since the one-voice configurations of the foreground represent several voices, it is not difficult to perceive the bass progressions hidden in the settings .... Particularly in fugue subjects it is most important to understand the implied bass formula. It ⟨ determines the countersubject and ⟩ pervades the entire fugue." (The inserted words are by Ernst Oster.) Schenker refers the reader to his study of the Fugue in *C* minor from the *Well-Tempered Clavier*, Book I, in *Meisterwerk*, II, pp. 55-95, which forms the main body of his essay "Das Organische der Fuge" mentioned by Jonas above.

Near the start of this essay, Schenker traces the idea that a fugue subject carries with it an implicit bass line to Marpurg's *Abhandlung von der Fuge* (1753-54; 2nd ed., 1806); partial translation in Alfred Mann, *The Study of Fugue* (New Brunswick: Rutgers University Press, 1958), pp. 139-212. Schenker quotes Marpurg's directives for composing a fugue subject, which include the injunction that one should "imagine the course of the bass and that of the other parts while working on the theme"; see *Meisterwerk*, II, p. 62 (English translation, p. 255; see also Mann, p. 163). A direct reference to Marpurg's treatise is found on a sheet containing a later graph of the opening of the Fugue, one of a group of loose sheets in the Oster Collection (see note 47 above). This sheet is reproduced in a facsimile that precedes the Translator's Foreword (plate I). The upper right corner contains a reference to p. 54 of Marpurg's treatise (2nd ed.); the numbers "XXV, 3" refer to the table in which Marpurg reproduces the Fugue of the Chromatic Fantasy, bars 1-19, as an example of an answer to a chromatic subject (see Mann, p. 174).

The rest of the sheet is devoted to a graph of the fugue subject, given in three levels. As was his usual practice, Schenker wrote the foreground graph first; it appears on the fifth staff of the sheet, numbered "3." and labeled "Fuge / Thema:" (the bass tones on the sixth staff were probably added later). The middleground level is found on the second and third staves, numbered "2." and annotated between the staves with the words "kons[onanter] dg [Durchgang]" (consonant passing tone) in parentheses and the remark "zur Beheb[ung] d[es] Sprung[es]" (for the elimination of the leap). The annotation "kons[onanter] dg [Durchgang] wegen 1. Mittelst[imme]" (consonant passing tone because of the first middle voice) appears to the right of the middleground graph. The background graph was to have been written at the top of the page but, lacking sufficient space, Schenker wrote it in the boxed lower right quarter of the page, keying it with the number "1." and the symbol "⊖". This graph is headed "S Bach Chrom[atische] Ph[antasie]." The word "Gliederung" (structural division) appears in parentheses to the right of the top voice; the annotation "2 Brch. [Brechungen]" (two arpeggiations) appears to the right of the bass. The word "Klang" found at the top of the page would seem to refer to the underlying composed-out triad. (The translator is indebted to John Rothgeb, who deciphered Schenker's annotations and clarified the details of the graphs.)

These sketches, which appear closely related to the graph given in *Der freie Satz*, were probably made in the late 1920s—one of the sheets in this group is a set of annotations written on the back of a gas bill dated 1928. These annotations include the following comment on the graph: "composed-out triad (*Klang*) (I) III V I." This remark, and of course the graphs themselves, show a direct line of development from Schenker's earlier thoughts on the fugal theme found at this point in the present study.]

*68. Cf. also bars 72 and 74.

[69. This "jargon" is nowhere in evidence in Schenker's personal copy; he placed the following letters and numbers below bars 9-12 of the score:]

bars:	9	10	11	12
	$D^7 \longrightarrow$	$G \; {}^{\sharp 7}_{\;4}$	$\natural 3$	$(A) \quad D$
D minor:	I $\quad {}^{\sharp 3}$	IV $\; {}^{2}$		I

*70. Cf. also the commentary to bar 8.

*71. See the commentary to bar 10.

*72. Cf. Schenker, *Kontrapunkt*, I, p. 276 ff.

[73. Bars 27-31.]

*74. Cf. Schenker, *Harmonielehre*, table 13 [in §140, p. 346 (English translation p. 236, tables omitted). The table shows that IV may be tonicized by the two chords that precede it in the circle of descending fifths: V-I-IV = II$^{(b3)}$-V-I.]

*75. The technique of using passing tones and anticipations to bring about such "diminutions" is discussed in Schenker, *Harmonielehre*, p. 404 f. [§164 (English translation, p. 306 ff.)], and in *Kontrapunkt*, I, p. 247 ff. [See especially Schenker's discussion of the use of passing dissonances, pp. 248-75.]

*76. Seen later at bars 60 and 91.

*77. Cf. Schenker, *Kontrapunkt*, I, p. 248 ff. and p. 312 ff.

[78. See, for example, Schenker, *Kontrapunkt*, II, pp. 205-6, a discussion of the resolution of a suspension at the second half note when second and fourth species are combined in three-voice writing. (Schenker uses the word *Fortbewegung*.) Most of this passage appears in translation in William Clark, "Heinrich Schenker on the Nature of the Seventh Chord," *Journal of Music Theory*, vol. 26, no. 2 (1982), pp. 234-35.]

[79. Brahms, *Variations and Fugue on a Theme by Handel*, Fugue, bar 33. Schenker reiterates these remarks in his extensive analysis of this work published in Heft 8/9 of *Der Tonwille* (cf. p. 32, discussion of the Fugue, bars 31-40). See Appendix: Works of Heinrich Schenker.]

*80. Cf. Schenker, *Harmonielehre*, §45 [pp. 113-15 (English translation, pp. 90-93)].

*81. Cf. Schenker, *Harmonielehre*, §176 [pp. 431-36 (English translation, pp. 328-29] and table 11 [p. 346. The English translation omits this table, which shows how each scale degree may be tonicized by the degree that lies a fifth above it.]

*82. And to think that all of this completely eluded Bülow, as he took it upon himself to correct Bach! Perhaps one will now finally understand why Brahms had to deny Bülow the approbation he so eagerly sought. [Schenker may have been alluding to Brahms's view that a memorial monument to Bülow should not be errected in Hamburg, since the conductor had made no lasting contribution to music. This subject had figured in Schenker's correspondence at the time he was preparing the present study. See Karl Grunsky's letter to Schenker, transcribed by Hellmut Federhofer in "Heinrich Schenkers Bruckner-Verständnis," *Archiv für Musikwissenschaft*, vol. 39, no. 3 (1982), p. 206, footnote 12; and Max Kalbeck, *Johannes Brahms*, vol. 4/2 (Berlin: Deutsche Brahms-Gesellschaft, 1914), pp. 371-72.]

[83. The tie is present in the BG edition, Schenker's source. It is absent in the Henle edition.]

*84. Cf. the discussion of bar 126. [In Schenker's personal copy, lower voices are added to example 49; these, combined with a sketch found in the margin of the score at bar 84 ff., yield the reconstruction shown in example L.

Example L

The score itself is heavily annotated; the 5-6 motion is indicated under the lower staves.]

[85. Schenker had listed bar 85 among the corrections of the BG edition given in his introduction; *G♯* is marked in his own copy for the printer to follow. The preface to the BG edition, p. xlvi, lists the reading of *G♯* as a variant. The Henle edition has *G♮*.]

[86. See the commentary to bar 27.]

[87. In Schenker's personal copy, a change is made in the bass scheme of example 50: at bar 88, the letter *E* is crossed out and is replaced with *G♯* in parentheses. The 5-6 motion is indicated under the letters. These changes conform to the following letters and numbers found under the left-hand part in the annotated score:

bars:	87		88		89	
	C	*(A)*	*B♮*	*(G♯)*	*A*	*(F♯)*
	5	6	5	6	5	6

(See also the sketch of bars 84-90, note 84 above).]

*88. Cf. Schenker, *Kontrapunkt*, I, p. 88 ff. and p. 120. [See especially pp. 91-94, where Schenker presents examples of melodies that show the use of the seventh as the inversion of the second.]

*89. Cf. Schenker, *Kontrapunkt*, I, §28! [pp. 226-31].

*90. Cf. my commentary to bar 41 and bar 60.

[91. *Einer kontinualen Mehrstimmigkeit*, i.e., like the added voices a continuo player would use—voices added as fillers to thicken the texture. The meaning ascribed to the word *kontinual* is perhaps clarified by Schenker's use of it as follows: "... gehe man sorgfältig der Natur des Klaviersatzes nach, die hier in so unendlich feinen Quantitäten die *obligaten und kontinualen Stimmen* mischt. (... one should carefully observe the idiomatic keyboard writing that mixes *essential and filling voices* in such infinitely delicate quantities.)" (translator's italics) See Schenker, *Die letzten fünf Sonaten von Beethoven, Sonate E dur Op. 109, Erläuterungsausgabe*, p. 27; revised ed., p. 6 (see Appendix: Works of Heinrich Schenker).]

[92. Schenker mistakenly listed the Busoni edition here (Busoni does not add the $b\natural^1$). The preface to the BG edition (p. xlvii) comments that the reading given by Bischoff and Bülow is not found in a single manuscript source.]

[93. See the seventh bar of the seventh entrance in table I.]

[94. *Die kontinuale Vollgriffigkeit.* See note 91 above.]

[95. Bars 68-75.]

*96. Cf. bar 84 ff. [The reference is to the chromatic descent from bar 84 depicted in example 49.]

[97. *Der Ausbruch kontinualer Mehrstimmigkeit.* See note 91 above.]

*98. In spite of its characterization as a "free ending," one should not overlook the fact that this measure is essentially based on the closing notes of the subject [example M]. (Jonas)

Example M

*99. Cf. C.P.E. Bach, *Versuch*, Part I, chapter 2, section 3, §14 [p. 75 (English translation, pp. 103-4)] and Schenker, *Ein Beitrag zur Ornamentik*, pp. 37-38 [English translation, pp. 76-79, "The Trill at a Dotted Note"].

[100. *BWV* 545, the last two measures of the Fugue.]

*101. Peters Edition no. 222, 2. [The Prelude and Fugue in *C* major is the second work included in vol. 1 of J. S. Bach, *Sechs Präludien und Fugen für Orgel*, transcribed by Franz Liszt (Leipzig: C. F. Peters, 1888). Liszt reproduces Bach's original notation for the closing bars of the Fugue, adding only the three-note suffix.]

*102. In table II, the numbers in parentheses at the words "subject" and "answer" serve to enumerate the entrances.

[103. Schenker gives the figures $\frac{8}{5}$ at the tenth entrance; this appears to be a misprint, which has been corrected to read $\frac{8}{3}$.]

[104. This statement, signed "Raro," is found in a collection of aphorisms by the imaginary Davidsbündler: "Aus Meister Raros, Florestans und Eusebius' Denk- und Dichtbüchlein." See Robert Schumann, *Gesammelte Schriften über Musik und Musikern* (5th ed.; Breitkopf & Härtel, 1914; reprinted, Westmead: Gregg, 1969), vol. 1, p. 24. Schenker was to cite this same remark again in the introduction to his essay "Das Organische der Fuge," *Meisterwerk*, II, p. 58; its characterization there as "Schumann-Caros Wort" is a misprint—Schenker must have intended "Schumann-*Raros* Wort." Schenker begins the essay with another quotation from Schumann's writings pertaining to fugal composition, a review of Mendelssohn's

Preludes and Fugues, op. 35 (see Schumann, *Gesammelte Schriften*, vol. 1, pp. 252-54). Schumann himself prepared a "Lehrbuch der Fugenkomposition"; see Schumann, *Gesammelte Schriften*, vol. 1, facsimile appearing between p. 470 and p. 471, and Wolfgang Boetticher, *Robert Schumann* (Berlin: Bernhard Hahnefeld, 1941), pp. 614-15.]

[105. A somewhat different evaluation of the fugal writing of these composers is found in Schenker, *Der freie Satz*, §322, pp. 215-17 (English translation, pp. 143-44).]

*106. A more detailed discussion of non-legato touch may be found in Schenker, *Ein Beitrag zur Ornamentik*, pp. 21-22 (English translation, pp. 46-47].

[107. Performance indications for the use of this technique at arpeggios and broken chords in the Fantasy were supplied by many editors, beginning with Griepenkerl (see, for example, bar 27 in the Peters edition). Directions are found in Schenker's personal copy, at the written-out arpeggio of bars 27-29. Schenker indicated that the first four tones of each arpeggiation be sustained by leaving the fingers on the keys; these tones are then further sustained by the pedal, which is held for the rest of the measure. This combination of "hand pedal" and foot pedal lends lightness and clarity to the performance of the arpeggios. Schenker's markings at bar 27 are shown in example N (the markings are repeated in the succeeding bars).

Example N

bar 27

Schenker's personal copies of the Beethoven sonatas (housed in the Oswald Jonas Memorial Collection at the University of California at Riverside) contain similar indications; highly significant examples were presented by William Rothstein in his paper, "Heinrich Schenker as an Interpreter of Beethoven's Piano Sonatas," read at the National Conference of the Society for Music Theory, Ann Arbor, Michigan, November 1982. Rothstein also described the discussion of "hand pedal" found in Schenker's unfinished treatise on performance (see note 111 below).]

*108. Cf. Schenker, *Ein Beitrag zur Ornamentik*, p. 9! [English translation, pp. 25-26].

[109. See note 2 above.]

*110. See, for example Quantz, *Versuch*, chapter 17, sections 2, 6, 7, etc. [pp. 187-206, 223-38, 239-74 (English translation, pp. 215-37, 250-65, 266-94)], or C.P.E. Bach, *Versuch*, Part I, chapter 3 [pp. 115-33 (English translation, pp. 147-66). Especially relevant here is Quantz's treatment of dynamics found in §§12-16 of his section 6 (English translation, pp. 254-59) where, after giving the general directive that dissonances are to be played louder than consonances, he prescribes specific gradations of *forte* for various types of dissonances; also pertinent is C.P.E. Bach's discussion in §29 of his chapter on performance (English translation, pp. 162-64), where he counters Quantz's theory by stating his belief that shading is dependent on individual contexts.]

The subject of dynamics is given such a valid psychological foundation in these treatises; the few directives given by the authors—for they aimed to impart only the most basic principles—are so beautifully delineated. The actual performance practice of the masters themselves must have far exceeded such directives!

[111. Schenker developed this idea in his monograph on Beethoven's Ninth Symphony (published two years after the present study; see Appendix: Works of Heinrich Schenker). In the preface, Schenker expresses his belief that dynamic symbols, far from being arbitrary, are predetermined by the inner content of a composition (see p. xiv). This important idea was also expressed in his incomplete work, "Die Kunst des Vortrags," which dates from this period. (Schenker mentions it in the same preface, p. xii.) See Oswald Jonas, "Die Kunst des Vortrages nach Heinrich Schenker," *Musikerziehung*, vol. 15, no. 3 (March 1962), pp. 127-29. Jonas owned and intended to publish the manuscript of Schenker's monograph on performance, along with related materials. These documents are now housed in the Jonas Collection. (Jonas's edition of "Die Kunst des Vortrags," completed by Heribert Esser, is in press at Universal Edition; a translation by Irene Schreier Scott is planned.) A valuable discussion of the materials in the Jonas Collection and their relationship to Schenker's ideas on performance was presented in William Rothstein's paper, "Heinrich Schenker as an Interpreter of Beethoven's Piano Sonatas." See also Charles Burkhart's important article, "Schenker's Theory of Levels and Musical Performance," in *Aspects of Schenkerian Theory*, ed. by David Beach (New Haven: Yale University Press, 1983), pp. 95-112.]

[112. Schenker reproduced the dynamic signs given in the BG edition (found only in the Fantasy) and added his own dynamic markings to both the Fantasy and the Fugue. (He had intended that his own dynamic signs be placed in parentheses; see the Preface and notes 1-2 above.) A somewhat similar situation exists in Schenker's earlier edition of C.P.E. Bach's keyboard works (see Appendix: Works of Heinrich Schenker), where he also added some of his own dynamic markings to those of the composer, though even more sparingly than in the present edition since a greater number of original indications were present. One might question the inclusion of editorial dynamic markings by an editor who did so much to promote fidelity to the composer's original text. Schenker's quest for authenticity, however, was always coupled with a concern for the performer. In the companion volume to his C.P.E. Bach edition, *Ein Beitrag zur Ornamentik* (p. 13; English translation, pp. 31-32), he had voiced this concern as follows:

> If I have added (in parentheses) a few of my own dynamic signs to Bach's inspired indications, it was not because I felt that there was a dearth of such signs. Rather, I feared that the performer, who might find the organization of the musical material difficult to grasp, would find Bach's signs insufficient and

would wish for more. This would be especially true if he were used to the large number of dynamic indications so patronizingly offered him in present-day editions.

In his later editions of the Beethoven sonatas, Schenker (with very few exceptions) included only the original markings, believing the composer's own indications to be entirely sufficient.

Schenker's views on superfluous printed dynamic markings are expressed in *Ein Beitrag zur Ornamentik*, p. 13, footnote 1 (English translation, p. 32, footnote 17):

> The eye of the player reacts automatically to all the signs that it encounters while reading the notes. The visual detour necessitated by a superfluous sign added by an editor might cause the hand to play something in excess of what it would have played without the editor's indication. When a player decides, of his own accord, upon some indefinable nuance of dynamics or rhythm impelled during performance, this is quite a different matter from his purely optical reaction to a fixed editorial sign. The principal fault of such a sign is its unequivocal presence—which lends it a factual existence it does not indeed possess.

Schenker entered some dynamic markings into his personal copy of the Chromatic Fantasy and Fugue, but these are clearly in a different category from those that appeared in print: they represent shadings which he felt should be suggested by the inner content of the music itself and not by external directives. For example, the markings he added to the *pf* (*poco forte*) found at the opening of the Fugue (see example O) give dynamic emphasis to the less stable elements of the underlying structure (see Schenker's graph in example K, note 67 above).

Example O

Comparable indications are added in the printed score only at some of the later entrances, which require bolder shading because of the competing voices.]

*113. For example, Beethoven's Ninth Symphony, first movement, bar 15 ff., bar 50 ff., bar 150 ff., and the *Andante maestoso* of the Finale [bars 1-16], etc. [Schenker examines these same measures in his monograph on the Ninth Symphony; see pp. 16-17, pp. 19-20, p. 67, and p. 325. His discussion of the performance of *forte* often recalls the present study, as in the following passage: "A lengthy stretch of *ff* begins at bar 150, yet those notes that Beethoven marked *sf* (bars 150, 151, 152) or simply *f* (bars 155-157) must even here be particularly emphasized—which is possible only if one plays the preceding tones with less force." (p. 67)] See also Brahms, Symphony no. 1, first movement, at the closing idea [bars 472-474], and in the coda [bars 503-507]. One may also recall the inspired, incredibly effective *piano* heard 31 bars before the end of Beethoven's Seventh Symphony [bar 435], a *piano* that is set into a dynamic plane of high intensity (beginning 39 bars before the end of the Symphony [in bar 427]). I would also recommend an examination of Brahms's Rhapsody in *G* minor [op. 79, no. 2]—a highly instructive illustration.

[114. Quoted in the *Vossische Zeitung* (also titled *Königlich privilegirte Berlinische Zeitung von Staats- und gelehrten Sachen*), no. 153 (April 3, 1907, morning edition), in an article by Franz Fridberg, found on the newspaper's second page under the heading "Feuilleton," and entitled "Erinnerungen an Johannes Brahms: Zum 10. Todestage des Meisters." Fridberg prints the entire text of the letter cited by Schenker, and explains that it was written in reply to a query from Brahms's friend Adolf Brodsky, a well-known violinist and professor at the Leipzig Conservatory (he had often performed Brahms's Violin Concerto). The letter (which does not seem to have been printed in any other source) is not dated, but it was probably written soon after the completion of the *G*-major Quintet in 1890. Brodsky, who was apparently preparing a performance of the Quintet from the manuscript, had asked Brahms if the *forte* indication for the two violins and two violas was correct, since it caused the upper instruments to obscure the opening cello solo. This same question had been the subject of much discussion among musicians involved in the work's early performances; see Kalbeck, *Johannes Brahms*, vol. 4/1, pp. 208-9, and Karl Geiringer, *Brahms: His Life and Work* (2nd. ed.; London: Allen and Unwin, 1968), pp. 242-43. The cellist to whom the remarks in Brahms's letter are addressed is Julius Klengel, whose playing Brahms much admired (see Kalbeck, vol. 4/2, pp. 382-83). The remainder of Fridberg's article presents recollections of his student days at the Vienna Conservatory, especially of his encounters with Brahms during that time (probably in the 1880s).]

[115. It is possible that Schenker had in mind Nietzsche's essay, *The Case of Wagner* (1888), especially Sections 11 and 12, which Nietzsche summarizes as follows:

That the theater should not lord it over the arts.
That the actor should not seduce those who are authentic.
That music should not become an art of lying.

See Friedrich Nietzsche, *The Birth of Tragedy and the Case of Wagner*, translated by Walter Kaufmann (New York: Vintage, 1967), p. 180.]

[116. "One should not sing with the voice, but with the heart"; the reference here may be to Saint Jerome.]

*117. See Brahms's words in my earlier citation [from the *Vossische Zeitung*].

*118. Particularly relevant here is Schenker, *Ein Beitrag zur Ornamentik*, pp. 12-13! [English translation, pp. 30-32].

[119. The clues to interpretation provided by Schenker's fingerings are discussed by Carl Schachter in his introduction to Schenker's edition of the complete Beethoven piano sonatas, pp. viii-ix. (See Appendix: Works of Heinrich Schenker.) See also Burkhart, "Schenker's Theory of Levels and Musical Performance," pp. 97-99.]

[120. The ensuing four items were not enumerated by Schenker; they were grouped together in one paragraph and each item was introduced by the word "oder" (or), which has been omitted in the translation.]

[121. The bar numbers cited in this section contained a series of typographical errors; an attempt has been made to correct such misprints here, as elsewhere.]

[122. Schenker's personal copy contains a few added or altered fingerings—some as alternative fingerings and others as corrections. In several cases the new fingerings apply to passages that may have seemed puzzling to performers using Schenker's edition. Selected examples are given below:

Fantasy

Bar 2, first and second quarters, when the right hand takes over: $\overset{2\,3}{1\,3}$ 4 3 2 1 3 2 (instead of 1 [2] 3 [2] 1 4 3 2). The highest note, g^2, is marked *piano*; the word "hoch" is added, presumably indicating a high position of the hand, to effect lightness of touch.

Bar 21, second quarter, right hand: 1 3 4 (instead of 1 [2] 3). The highest note, bb^2, is marked *piano* and *diminuendo* (after a *crescendo* approach).

Both of the above fingerings show Schenker's use of 1 3 4 (in conjunction with dynamic markings), to de-emphasize a melodic high note. Schenker's sketch of the opening bars of the Fantasy (see example J in note 47 above) provides an explanation for the first example; the g^2 is regarded as an embellishing tone. In the second example, Schenker may have wished to allow the harmonic tones and the rhythmic grouping to emerge from the pitches themselves, without additional dynamic emphasis (see note 31 above).

Bar 78, third quarter, right hand: 5 $\widehat{43}$ (instead of 4 3) for the two eighth notes, written in the margin like a correction of proof. This alteration shows Schenker's characteristic use of the silent change of finger at the end of a slur, as seen in the printed fingerings in the preceding bars 76 and 77.

Fugue

Bars 19-20, left hand: the fingering 5 4 3 2 is given for the quarter notes a-bb-$b\natural$-c^1.

Bar 20, first quarter, right hand: $\widehat{15}$. This change of finger is necessary if the g^1 is to be held for its full value.

Bar 22, first quarter: the brace that connects the tones of the middle and lower voices is marked with a delete symbol, indicating that the d^1 should be played with the right hand instead of the left; the left hand may thus play the bass tones e-f-$f\sharp$-g (starting in bar 21) with the corrrected fingering 5 4 3 2.

The new fingerings in bars 19-22 appear in the margin as well as at the notes themselves; written in red pencil, they are clearly intended as corrections.

Bars 36-37, right hand: a silent change from 4 to 5 is indicated for the dotted half note f^1 in bar 36. In bar 37 the fingering 5 4 at f^1 and e^1 is replaced, in the margin, by 4 5.

Bar 38: the fingering 2 1 3 is suggested for the second, third, and fourth eighth notes in the left hand. This, as well as the fingering $\widehat{21}$ for the $b\natural$ in the middle voice suggests that the right hand, not the left, should play the $b\natural$.

Bar 111, right hand: the printed fingering for the trill, 3 5 changing to 3 4 at the second quarter, is altered to the more logical succession 3 4 to 3 5; the correction is entered in the margin as well as at the trill itself.

Bar 117, last quarter, right hand: f^2-e^2 is fingered 5 3; this necessitates the use of 2 3 5 (instead of 2 3 4) in approaching the melodic high note f^2, effecting a more subtle emphasis.]

[123. *Das Fortspinnenkönnen des Tones.*]

*124. See the fingering given in Schumann's *Studien für das Pianoforte, nach Capricen von Paganini*, op. 3, no. 3, which Schumann characterizes in his preface as follows: "[I] call attention to the silent exchange of the fingers on a single key that often (even more than here) produces a beautiful effect in an adagio." [Robert Schumann, *Werke*, ed. by Clara Schumann and Johannes Brahms (Leipzig: Breitkopf & Härtel, 1881-93), Series VII/1, p. 38. Opus 3 (pp. 30-35) is preceded by its own preface; the sentence quoted by Schenker appears on p. 25.]

*125. Michael Praetorius, *Syntagma Musicum*, [vol. 2: *De Organographia* (1618). See *Publikation älterer praktischer und theoretischer Musikwerke*, vol. 13 (Leipzig: Breitkopf & Härtel, 1884 and 1894; reprinted New York: Broude Brothers, 1966), and the facsimile of the 2nd ed. (1619) issued by Wilibald Gurlitt (Kassel: Bärenreiter, 1929 and 1958). Also cited in Spitta, *Johann Sebastian Bach*, vol. 1, p. 645 (English translation, vol. 2, p. 34).]

*126. See the BG or "Urtext" edition. [Bach provided fingering for three keyboard pieces. The first, *BWV* 994, is no. 1 (Applicatio) in the *Clavier-Büchlein* for Wilhlem Friedemann; it may be found in the BG edition, vol. 36 (the same volume that contains the Chromatic Fantasy and Fugue), Anhang 2, p. 237; see also J. S. Bach, *Neue Ausgabe sämtlicher Werke* (*NBA*), Series V/5 (Kassel: Bärenreiter, 1962), p. 4 and p. viii (facsimile). The second piece, *BWV* 930, is no. 9 (Praeambulum) of the *Clavier-Büchlein*, BG edition, vol. 36, pp. 126-27 (no. 11 of the *Zwölf kleine Praeludien*); see also *NBA*, Series V/5, pp. 12-13. The third piece (*BWV* 870a) is an early version of the *C*-major Prelude and Fugue in Book II of the *Well-Tempered Clavier*, BG edition, vol. 36, Anhang 1, pp. 224-25. Arnold Dolmetsch reproduces these pieces and presents an analysis of the fingering, focusing on the second piece. See *The Interpretation of the Music of the Seventeenth and Eighteenth Centuries* (Seattle: University of Washington Press, 1969; reprint of the edition of 1915, revised 1946), pp. 412-18, and appendix (published separately). Schenker was no doubt familiar with the discussion of the first two pieces given in Spitta, *Johann Sebastian Bach*, vol. 1, pp. 649-650 and Beilage 3a and 3b (English translation, vol. 2, p. 39 and vol. 3, pp. 385-86).]

*127. See especially Gustav Nottebohm, *Zweite Beethoveniana* [Leipzig: J. Rieter-Biedermann, 1887], chapter 37, p. 356 ff.! [In his personal copy of the present study, at the bottom of the last page of the text, Schenker lists several sonatas that contain examples of Beethoven's fingerings: op. 2, no. 1 (Trio of the Menuetto), op. 2, no. 2 (first movement), op. 2, no. 3 (last movement), op. 53, (last movement), op. 101 (last movement), op. 110, and op. 111. His list also includes the Diabelli Variations (variation 8), and the Six Variations in *F* major, op. 34 (variation 2). Beethoven's own fingerings have been the subject of several studies; among the more recent are Jeanne Bamberger, "The Musical Significance of Beethoven's Fingerings in the Piano Sonatas," *The Music Forum*, vol. 4 (New York: Columbia University Press, 1976), pp. 237-80, and William S. Newman, "Beethoven's Fingerings as Interpretive Clues," *The Journal of Musicology*, vol. 1, no. 2 (1982), pp. 171-97.]

*128. What delicacies one finds in Chopin's etudes, for example in no. 18 and no. 27; see the "Urtext" edition. [The reference is to the Etude in *G♯* minor, op. 25, no. 6, and to the Etude in *D♭* major from the *Trois nouvelles Etudes*, in Chopin, *Werke*, ed. by Woldemar Bargiel, Johannes Brahms, August Franchomme, Franz Liszt, Carl Reinecke, and Ernst Rudorff (Leipzig: Breitkopf & Härtel, 1878-80), vol. 2, pp. 63-67 and pp. 98-99. Schenker may be alluding to the fingering in bars 43-46 (left hand) of the *G♯*-minor Etude and that in bars 69-71 of the *D♭*-major Etude; in both places Chopin indicates that the thumb should play several notes in succession. There is some controversy about the latter passage, however, since Chopin's vertical stroke could be interpreted as either the number one or as a staccato mark.]

*129. Schumann's Paganini studies! [see note 124 above].

*130. Brahms, *51 Übungen*! [Berlin: Simrock, 1893].

Appendix

Works of Heinrich Schenker

The following is a list of Schenker's major publications, both in the original German as well as in English editions and translations. The German publications marked with an asterisk are in print.[1]

Ein Beitrag zur Ornamentik. Vienna: Universal Edition, 1904.
> *Revised and enlarged edition, 1908. (See also under English translations.)

Neue musikalische Theorien und Phantasien.
> Vol. I: *Harmonielehre*. Stuttgart: Cotta, 1906.
>> *Reprint, with a foreword by Rudolf Frisius. Vienna: Universal Edition, 1978. (See also under English translations.)
>
> Vol. II, Part I: *Kontrapunkt I*. Vienna: Universal Edition, 1910.
>> Part II: *Kontrapunkt II*. Vienna: Universal Edition, 1922.
>
> Vol. III: *Der freie Satz*. Vienna: Universal Edition, 1935.
>> *Second edition, edited and revised by Oswald Jonas. Vienna: Universal Edition, 1956. (See also under English translations.)

J. S. Bach, Chromatische Phantasie und Fuge: kritische Ausgabe. Vienna: Universal Edition, 1910.
> *Revised edition by Oswald Jonas. Vienna: Universal Edition, 1969. (See also under English translations.)

Beethovens neunte Sinfonie. Vienna: Universal Edition, 1912.
> *Reprint. Vienna: Universal Edition, 1969.

---

1. A complete, comprehensive, carefully annotated list of Schenker's writings is to be found in David Beach, "A Schenker Bibliography," *Journal of Music Theory*, vol. 13, no. 1 (1969), pp. 2-37; reprinted in *Readings in Schenker Analysis*, ed. by Maury Yeston (New Haven: Yale University Press, 1977), pp. 275-311; and supplemented by "A Schenker Bibliography: 1969-1979," *Journal of Music Theory*, vol. 23, no. 2 (1979), pp. 275-86. This bibliography also includes the most important books, monographs, and articles by other authors. For a valuable guide to the location of Schenker's analyses in his writings, see Larry Laskowski, *Heinrich Schenker: An Annotated Index to his Analyses of Musical Works* (New York: Pendragon Press, 1978).

Erläuterungsausgabe der letzten fünf Sonaten Beethovens. Vienna: Universal Edition.
  Op. 109, published 1913.
  Op. 110, published 1914.
  Op. 111, published 1915.
  Op. 101, published 1920.
  (Op. 106 was never published.)
  *New edition of Op. 101, 109, 110, 111, revised by Oswald Jonas. Vienna: Universal Edition, 1971-72.
Der Tonwille, 10 issues. Vienna: A. Gutmann Verlag, 1921-24. Later republished in three volumes by Universal Edition.
Beethovens fünfte Sinfonie (reprinted from *Der Tonwille*). Vienna: Universal Edition, 1925.
  *Reprint. Vienna: Universal Edition, 1969. (See also under English translations.)
Das Meisterwerk in der Musik. Munich: Drei Masken Verlag.
  Jahrbuch I, published 1925.
  Jahrbuch II, published 1926.
  Jahrbuch III, published 1930.
  *Reprint (three volumes in one). Hildesheim: Georg Olms Verlag, 1974. (See also under English translations.)
Fünf Urlinie-Tafeln. Vienna: Universal Edition, 1932. (See also under English translations.)
Johannes Brahms, Oktaven und Quinten u. a. Vienna: Universal Edition, 1933. (See also under English translations.)

Editions of Music

Ph. Em. Bach, Klavierwerke (selections). Vienna: Universal Edition, 1902.
Beethoven, Klaviersonaten: nach den Autographen und Erstdrucken rekonstruiert. Vienna: Universal Edition, 1921-23.
  *New edition, revised by Erwin Ratz. Vienna: Universal Edition, 1945-47. (See also under English editions.)
Beethoven, Sonata, Op. 27, Nr. 2. Facsimile, with an introduction by Schenker. Vienna: Universal Edition, 1921.

English Editions and Translations

J. S. Bach's Chromatic Fantasy and Fugue: Critical Edition with Commentary. Translated and edited by Hedi Siegel. New York: Longman Inc., 1984.
Beethoven, Complete Piano Sonatas. Reprint of the edition of 1921-23, with an introduction by Carl Schachter. New York: Dover, 1975.
"[Beethoven, Symphony No. 5: Analysis of the First Movement]." Translated by Elliot Forbes and F. John Adams, Jr. In *Beethoven, Symphony No. 5 in C minor* (Norton Critical Scores). New York: Norton, 1971.

"Brahms's Study, Octaven u. Quinten u. A.," with commentary by Schenker. Translated and annotated by Paul Mast. In *The Music Forum*, vol. 5. New York: Columbia University Press, 1980.

"A Contribution to the Study of Ornamentation." Translated by Hedi Siegel. In *The Music Forum*, vol. 4. New York: Columbia University Press, 1976.

Five Graphic Music Analyses. Reprint of *Fünf Urlinie-Tafeln*, with an introduction by Felix Salzer. New York: Dover, 1969.

Free Composition. Translated and edited by Ernst Oster. New York: Longman Inc., 1979.

Harmony. Edited and annotated by Oswald Jonas. Translated by Elisabeth Mann Borgese. Chicago: University of Chicago Press, 1954. Reprint. Cambridge, Mass.: M.I.T. Press, 1973.

"The Largo of J. S. Bach's Sonata No. 3 for Unaccompanied Violin" (from *Das Meisterwerk in der Musik*, vol. 1). Translated by John Rothgeb. In *The Music Forum*, vol. 4. New York: Columbia University Press, 1976.

"Organic Structure in Sonata Form" (from *Das Meisterwerk in der Musik*, vol. 2). Translated by Orin Grossman. *Journal of Music Theory*, vol. 12 (1968). Reprinted in *Readings in Schenker Analysis*, edited by Maury Yeston. New Haven: Yale University Press, 1977.

"The Sarabande of J. S. Bach's Suite No. 3 for Unaccompanied Violoncello" (from *Das Meisterwerk in der Musik*, vol. 2). Translated by Hedi Siegel. In *The Music Forum*, vol. 2. New York: Columbia University Press, 1970.

ABOUT THE TRANSLATOR

Hedi Siegel was introduced to the theories of Heinrich Schenker by her mother, Elise Braun Barnett, and by Ernst Oster, a friend of her family. At Barnard College, and in the graduate program in musicology at Columbia University, she was a student of William J. Mitchell. As editorial assistant of *The Music Forum* since its inception, she has worked closely with Felix Salzer; she has also contributed translations of Schenker's writings, which were published in volumes 2 and 4. Her translation of Schenker's unpublished essay on thorough bass is in preparation for volume 6. Translations of the *Erläuterungsausgabe* of Beethoven's late piano sonatas are projected for the Longman series.

Currently, Hedi Siegel teaches music theory at Hunter College, where she is an adjunct Assistant Professor.